ALL ABOUT
PASTA & NOODLES

Joy of Cooking

ALL ABOUT
PASTA & NOODLES

IRMA S. ROMBAUER
MARION ROMBAUER BECKER
ETHAN BECKER

PHOTOGRAPHY BY LEIGH BEISCH

A Dorling Kindersley Book

Dorling DK Kindersley

LONDON, NEW YORK, SYDNEY, DELHI, PARIS, MUNICH AND JOHANNESBURG

First published in Great Britain in 2001 by
Dorling Kindersley Limited, 9 Henrietta Street, London WC2E 8PS

Published by arrangement with the original publisher,
Scribner, an imprint of Simon & Schuster, Inc.

WELDON OWEN INC.
Chief Executive Officer: John Owen
President: Terry Newell
Chief Operating Officer: Larry Partington
Vice President, International Sales: Stuart Laurence
Publisher: Roger Shaw
Creative Director: Gaye Allen
Associate Publisher: Val Cipollone
Art Director: Jamie Leighton
Production Director: Stephanie Sherman
Designer: Fiona Knowles
Consulting Editors: Norman Kolpas, Judith Dunham
Assistant Editor: Anna Mantzaris
Studio Manager: Brynn Breuner
Pre-press Coordinator: Mario Amador
Production Manager: Chris Hemesath
Food Stylist: Dan Becker Prop Stylist: Sara Slavin
Studio Assistant: Sheri Giblin
Food Styling Assistant: Jonathan Justus
Step-by-Step Photographer: Chris Shorten
Step-by-Step Food Stylist: Kim Brent

Joy of Cooking All About series was designed
and produced by Weldon Owen Inc.,
814 Montgomery Street, San Francisco,
California 94133, USA

Set in Joanna MT and Gill Sans

Reproduced by Bright Arts Singapore
Text film output by Mick Hodson Associates
Printed in Singapore by Tien Wah Press (Pte.) Ltd.

A CIP catalogue record for this book is available
from The British Library

ISBN 0 7513 3533 9

NOTE: Use either metric or imperial measurements since
conversions are not exact equivalents.

see our complete catalogue at
www.dk.com

Recipe shown on half-title page: *Potato Gnocchi, 124*
Photograph shown on title page: *Oriental Noodles, 92*

CONTENTS

FOREWORD

"When freshly cooked and tossed in or served with a meat, fish or cheese sauce, pasta needs only a salad to make a nutritious, inexpensive and quick meal." With those words in the Joy of Cooking, *my Granny Rom and my mother anticipated half a century ago how popular pasta and noodle dishes would become today.*

The enduring popularity of pasta and noodles inspires this volume of the new All About *series. You'll find instructions for making fresh pasta, information on key ingredients, sections on dumplings and Asian noodles, and recipes for basic stocks and sauces – everything you need whether you're cooking a casual family meal or a special dinner.*

You might notice that this collection of kitchen-tested recipes is adapted from the latest edition of the Joy of Cooking. *Just as our family has done for generations, we have worked to make this version of* Joy *a little bit better than the last. As a result, you'll find that some notes, recipes and techniques have been changed to improve their clarity and usefulness. Since 1931, the* Joy of Cooking *has constantly evolved. And now, the* All About *series has taken* Joy *to a whole new stage, as you will see from the beautiful colour photographs of finished dishes and clearly illustrated instructions for preparing and serving them. Granny Rom and Mother would have been delighted.*

I'm sure you'll find All About Pasta & Noodles *to be both a useful and an enduring companion in your kitchen.*

Enjoy!

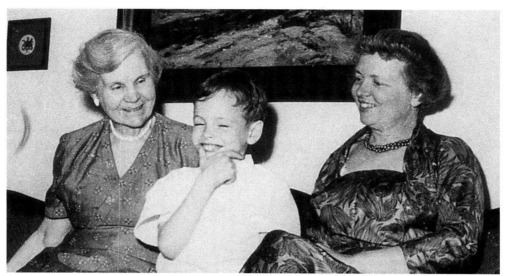

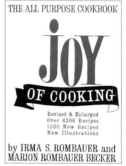

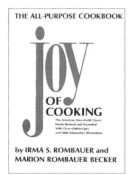

Ethan Becker pictured with his grandmother, Irma von Starkloff Rombauer (left), and his mother, Marion Rombauer Becker (right). Irma Rombauer published the first Joy of Cooking at her own expense in 1931. Marion Rombauer Becker became coauthor in 1951. Joy as it has progressed through the decades (from top left to bottom right): the 1931 edition with Marion's depiction of St. Martha of Bethany, said to be the patron saint of cooking, "slaying the dragon of kitchen drudgery"; the 1943 edition; the 1951 edition; the 1962 edition; the 1975 edition; and the 1997 edition.

About Pasta & Noodles

Nowhere is our tendency to mix and match world flavours more evident than in our passion for pasta and noodles, not to mention dumplings such as gnocchi and *Kartoffelklöse*. From linguine to lo mein, from spätzle to soba, pasta and noodles make up one of the largest and richest chapters in cooking all over the world. Certainly Italy has made the greatest contribution. That country's influence on our love affair with noodles is so great that the Italian word *pasta* has become a part of our everyday language. In this book, we use the word *pasta* to refer to noodles of Italian origin and *noodles* when referring to eastern European and Oriental dishes.

Dried and Fresh Pasta

Dried pasta and fresh pasta are not better or worse, only different. That venerable favourite, spaghetti, is always a dried pasta made of the strongest durum wheat and water, never eggs. On the other hand, fettuccine are flour and egg noodles that are best when fresh. However, in every case, a packet of good-quality dried pasta is far better than any mediocre fresh pasta. Although some high-quality fresh pastas are available, most cannot compare with what you can produce in your own kitchen. Making your own pasta provides the pleasure and satisfaction of working with your hands to master a craft, and the results make for memorable eating.

Cooking Pasta

Fresh or dried, pasta should always be cooked in a large quantity of fiercely boiling salted water. Use about 1 tablespoon salt per 3 litres (5 pints) water. Estimate 6 litres (10 pints) water per 500g (1lb) pasta, except for delicate filled pastas and very large noodles such as lasagne, which will need 9–12 litres (15–20 pints) water. In either case, cooking more than 1kg (2lb) of pasta at once invites problems of uneven cooking and draining.

Adequate water and frequent stirring are the two keys to eliminating the problem of pasta sticking together. Adding oil to the water has little effect except to keep the pot from boiling over. Do not break up pasta before cooking.

Since pasta cooks quickly and is at its best as soon as it is cooked, have everything ready before you start – the sauce prepared, a large colander set in the sink for draining, and a serving bowl and dishes warming in the oven. Once the salted water is rapidly boiling, add the pasta all at once. As soon as the pasta softens slightly, give it a stir, partially cover the pot and let it continue to boil vigorously, stirring often to keep it from sticking together.

Once the pasta tastes done, empty the pot immediately into the colander and quickly toss the colander to rid the pasta of as much water as possible. In a few recipes, some of the pasta water is ladled from the pot just before draining and blended into the sauce. Usually these are sauces based on sautés. The starch, salt and liquid extend the sauce and bring seasoning and body to it. Adding more oil would make the sauce too unctuous and heavy. The small amount of starch in the pasta water also encourages these light sauces to cling to the pasta.

Combine the drained pasta with its sauce over heat or simply toss the hot pasta and sauce in a warmed serving bowl. Rinse pasta only if it is destined to be baked or to be eaten cool in a salad. The starch helps the hot pasta meld with the sauce.

AL DENTE

Different pastas have different cooking times, and the only test for doneness is to lift a piece from the pot and taste it. Italians consider the ideal state *al dente* (to the tooth), which means tender but firm – no raw flour taste and enough firmness to give a pleasing resistance to the bite. Start testing fresh pasta and very thin shapes after about 30 seconds, spaghetti and linguine after 4 minutes and thick macaroni after 8 minutes.

RULES FOR COOKING PASTA

● Pasta should be cooked and eaten; never prepare it ahead. Cook and immediately toss with sauce.

● Count on 6 litres (5 pints) boiling water seasoned with about 1 tbsp salt per 500g (1lb) of pasta. Eliminate salt only if absolutely necessary. Delicate filled pastas or large pieces need 8-12 litres (15-20 pints) water. Do not use oil.

● Unless outrageously long, do not break pasta before cooking.

● Cook pasta at a fierce boil, stirring often. Fresh pasta cooks in several seconds to several minutes, while dried pasta takes longer. Taste for doneness. There should be no raw flour taste and some firmness to the bite (Italians call this *al dente*). Throw soft, mushy pasta out.

● Immediately drain cooked pasta into a large colander and toss to rid it of all water. Then quickly combine with sauce.

● Never rinse pasta unless it will be baked or served cool in a salad. Starches clinging to the surface of the noodles help them meld with the sauces.

● Pasta is best hot, so warm up its serving bowl and dishes if at all possible.

● Pasta salads are best cool or at room temperature, not cold.

Matching Pasta Shapes and Sauces

Italy claims at least three hundred different pasta shapes (some authorities assert as many as a thousand). With all these possibilities, it helps to remember a basic rule for pairing pasta and sauce – the chunkier and more robust the sauce, the bolder the pasta shape. Hollow maccheroni, wide, thick lasagnette and broad ribbons of pappardelle take to sauces with big flavours and bite-sized chunks of vegetables or meats. Ethereal angel hair is best in soups or light sauces. Remember that pasta needs to be moistened with sauce, not drowned in it: you want to taste the pasta as well as the sauce. The same pasta may go by different names in different parts of Italy. A corkscrew shape may be called fusilli or rotelle; filled square or rectangular pastas are tortelli in some areas, agnolotti in others and ravioli elsewhere.

Guide to Italian Pasta Shapes and Uses

	shape & name	goes with	substitutions
	**Bucatini** *Little Mouths* cooking time: 10 to 18 minutes	**Chunky and/or robust sauces:** *Piquant Tomato Sauce, 36* *Fresh Tomato Sauce with* *Mozzarella, 39*	*Perciatelli* *Bigoli* *Sedani* *Long Fusilli*
	**Capelli d'Angelo/ Capellini** *Angel Hair* cooking time: 2 to 4 minutes	**Delicate, light sauces:** *Garlic and Oil, 50* *Butter and Cheese, 51* *Fresh Herbs, 53*	*Vermicelli* *Spaghettini*
	**Cavatelli** cooking time: 9 to 13 minutes	**Sauces with full flavours but not large pieces:** *Bolognese Sauce, 43* *Fresh Tomato Sauce, 39* *Prawns and Fresh Chilli* *Peppers, 55*	*Small Gnocchi* *Malloreddus* *Sedanini*

shape & name	goes with	substitutions

Conchiglie
Shells
cooking time:
8 to 20 minutes

Mini shells in soups
Small shells with sauces:
Sun-Dried Tomato Sauce, 36
Chicken Ragù, 44
Tomato Sauces, 31 to 47
Tuna Noodle Casserole, 86
Large stuffed shells:
All fillings, 66 to 67

Ziti
Penne
Fusilli
Orecchiette

Farfalle
Butterflies
or Bow Ties
cooking time:
9 to 12 minutes

Chunky sauces with bold flavours:
Spicy Chicken Bits and Broccoli, 45
Chicken Ragù, 44

Shells
Short Fusilli
Sedani
Penne

Fettuccine
Ribbons
cooking time:
7 to 9 minutes

Creamy sauces and chunky medium- to full-bodied sauces:
Fettuccine Alfredo, 51
Fresh Herbs, 53
Tomato Sauces, 31 to 47
Bolognese Sauce, 43
Chicken Ragù, 44

Tagliatelle

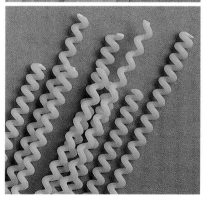

Fusilli
Corkscrews
cooking time:
Long: 8 to 12 minutes
Short: 10 to 15 minutes

Chunky sauces with bold flavours:
Long: *Porcini and Red Wine Sauce, 53*
Pesto Sauce, 52
Prawns and Fresh Chilli Peppers, 55
Short: *Baked Macaroni and Cheese, 88*
Tuna Noodle Casserole, 86

Penne
Bigoli
Bucatini
Sedani
Medium Shells
Farfalle
Rotelle

| shape & name | goes with | substitutions |

Gnocchi
Dumplings
cooking time:
Potato: 6 minutes
Semolina: Baked
25 minutes

Light to bold sauces:
Bolognese Sauce, 43
Chicken Ragù, 44
Tomato Sauces, 31 to 47
Butter and Cheese, 51
Porcini and Red Wine Sauce, 53

Potato: *Hollow and Shaped Maccheroni*
Semolina: *No substitutions*

Lasagne
cooking time:
8 to 14 minutes

Lasagne, 70 to 73

Maltagliati
Pappardelle

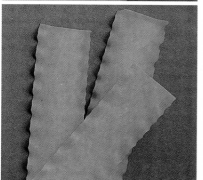

Lasagnette
Little Lasagne
cooking time:
9 to 15 minutes

Big, bold-flavoured sauces:
Bolognese Sauce, 43
Chicken Ragù, 44

Pappardelle
Maltagliati
Broken Lasagne

Linguine
Little Tongues
cooking time:
5 to 8 minutes

Smooth to chunky sauces, light to medium bodied:
Pesto Sauce, 52
Red Pesto Sauce, 52
Fresh Tomato Sauce, 39

Spaghetti
Trenette
Maccheroni alla Chitarra

shape & name	goes with	substitutions

Maccheroni alla Chitarra
Guitar Pasta
cooking time:
6 to 8 minutes

Medium- to full-bodied sauces:
Tomato Sauces, 31 to 47
Tinned Tuna Sauce, 57

Spaghetti
Bigoli

Maltagliati
Bad Cuts
cooking time:
2 to 5 minutes

Light to bold sauces:
Tomato Sauces, 31 to 47
Bolognese Sauce, 43
Chicken Ragù, 44

Broken:
   Pappardelle
For chunky sauces:
Broken Lasagne
Farfalle
Penne

Meloni
Melon Seeds
cooking time:
5 to 8 minutes

Soups

Orzo
Broken Spaghetti
Linguine
Vermicelli

Orecchiette
Little Ears
cooking time:
10 to 15 minutes

Bold, chunky sauces:
Sausage and Sprouting Broccoli, 60
Bolognese Sauce, 43
Chicken Ragù, 44
Piquant Tomato Sauce, 36

Shells
Farfalle

shape & name	goes with	substitutions

Orzo
Barley Kernels
cooking time:
10 to 13 minutes

Soups
Fresh Herbs, 53

Meloni

Pappardelle
cooking time:
9 to 13 minutes

Robust sauces:
Bolognese Sauce, 43
Puttanesca Sauce, 36

Lasagnette
Maltagliati
Broken Lasagne
Tagliatelle
Fettuccine

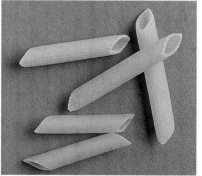

Penne
Quills or Pens
cooking time:
10 to 15 minutes

**Chunky sauces, casseroles,
tomato and vegetable sauces:**
Porcini and Red Wine Sauce, 53
Bolognese Sauce, 43

Sedani
Shells
Short Fusilli

Perciatelli
cooking time:
10 to 18 minutes

Chunky and/or robust sauces:
Piquant Tomato Sauce, 36
*Fresh Tomato Sauce with
    Mozzarella, 39*

Bucatini
Bigoli
Sedani
Long Fusilli

shape & name	goes with	substitutions

Pizzoccheri
Buckwheat Ribbons
cooking time:
10 to 14 minutes

Deep-flavoured, robust sauces:
Sausage and Sprouting Broccoli, 60

Wholemeal Pasta
Fettuccine
Tagliatelle
Pappardelle
Fusilli

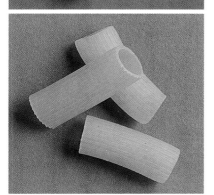

Rigatoni
Big Ribs
cooking time:
10 to 16 minutes

Sturdy sauces with big flavours:
Puttanesca Sauce, 36
Prawns and Fresh Chilli Peppers, 55

Ziti
Short Fusilli
Penne
Sedani
Strozzapreti

Sedani, Sedanini
Celery, Little Celery
cooking time:
8 to 14 minutes

Robust sauces and vegetable sauces:
Tinned Tuna Sauce, 57
Red Pesto Sauce, 52
Fresh Tomato Sauce with Black Olives, 39
Puttanesca Sauce, 36

Penne
Short Fusilli
Shells

Spaghetti
Little Strings
cooking time:
7 to 8 minutes

Medium-bodied sauces:
Tomato Sauces, 31 to 47
Puttanesca Sauce, 36
Classic Neapolitan Tomato Sauce II, 42

Linguine
Maccheroni alla Chitarra
Trenette

shape & name	goes with	substitutions

Tagliatelle
Little Cuts
cooking time:
7 to 10 minutes

Substantial sauces with chunky vegetables:
Bolognese Sauce, 43
Primavera, 54
Italian Tomato Sauce, 36

Fettuccine

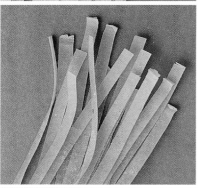

Trenette
cooking time:
7 to 10 minutes

As for Tagliatelle

Tagliatelle
Linguine

Vermicelli
Little Worms
cooking time:
4 to 6 minutes

Light sauces:
Butter and Cheese, 51
Garlic and Oil, 50
Fresh Herbs, 53

Capellini

Ziti
Bridegrooms
cooking time:
12 to 18 minutes

Big sauces with deep flavours:
Puttanesca Sauce, 36
Bolognese Sauce, 43
Prawns and Fresh Chilli
  Peppers, 55

Rigatoni
Broken Lasagne
Penne

Chicken Stock

About 2 litres (3¼ pints)

Stocks are the base for many pasta sauces. Using the lesser amount of chicken suggested below will result in a lighter stock; the greater amount will yield a richer one.

Combine in a stockpot over medium heat:

2–2.75kg (4–5½ lb) chicken parts (backs, necks, wings, legs or thighs), or 1 whole 2–2.75kg (4–5½ lb) roasting chicken, well rinsed

4 litres (6½ pt) cold water (or just enough to cover)

Bring to a boil, reduce the heat and simmer gently. Skim often until impurities no longer appear, about 30 minutes. Add:

1 onion, coarsely chopped

1 carrot, peeled and coarsely chopped

1 celery stalk, coarsely chopped

1 *Bouquet Garni*, below

Simmer, uncovered, for 3 hours, adding water as needed to cover. Strain into a clean pot or heatproof plastic container. Let cool, uncovered, then refrigerate. Remove the fat when ready to use.

Brown Beef Stock

About 2.5 litres (4 pints)

The combination of beef shanks and chicken bones produces a hearty stock.

Preheat the oven to 220°C (425°F) Gas 7. Lightly oil a roasting tin. Place in the prepared tin and roast for 15 minutes:

1.5kg (3lb) meaty beef shanks, cut into 5cm (2in) pieces, or oxtails, split into chunks, or a combination

Add:

500g (1lb) chicken parts (backs, necks, wings, legs or thighs), well rinsed

2 medium onions, quartered

2 carrots, peeled and thickly sliced

2 celery stalks, cut into 5cm (2in) pieces

Roast, stirring occasionally to prevent the vegetables from burning, until the bones are well browned, about 40 minutes. Transfer the meat and vegetables to a stockpot, carefully pour off any excess grease without discarding the caramelized cooking juices, and add to the hot roasting tin:

500ml (16floz) cold water

Scrape up any browned bits, then add the liquid to the pot along with:

3.5 litres (5½ pints) cold water (or just enough to cover)

Bring to a boil over medium heat, skim off the impurities, reduce the heat and simmer gently. Skim often until impurities no longer appear, about 30 minutes. Add:

1 leek, split lengthwise, cleaned and cut into 5cm (2in) pieces

1 *Bouquet Garni*, right, including 1 whole clove

Simmer, uncovered, for 4 hours, skimming as necessary and adding water as needed to cover. Strain into a clean pot or heatproof plastic container. Let cool, uncovered, then refrigerate. Remove the fat when ready to use.

Bouquet Garni

Since herbs tend to float and get in the way as you skim the surface of a stock, we recommend tying them together in a little packet, known as a bouquet garni. Vary the contents to suit your dish.

Wrap in a 10 × 10cm (4 × 4in) piece of muslin:

Small bunch of parsley or parsley stems

8 sprigs fresh thyme, or 1 tsp dried

1 bay leaf

2 or 3 celery leaves (optional)

Tie the muslin securely with a piece of thread or omit the muslin and simply tie the herbs together at their stems. Refrigerate in a tightly covered container until ready to use.

Cheese for Pasta

Seek out good Italian cheeses and always taste before buying. When good-quality imported Italian cheeses are not available, you can substitute domestic cheese. The trick is to keep the taste and sense of the cheese as close to the original as possible.

PARMIGIANO-REGGIANO
This mouth-filling cow's milk cheese with a complex and pleasing aftertaste is made in a small, legally designated area of Emilia-Romagna in northern Italy. It is the only true Parmesan. All the others are imitations. Older is *not* better. Today's Parmigiano-Reggiano usually reaches its peak at about two years. Before World War II, when different cows gave Parmigiano-Reggiano milk, the cheese successfully aged longer. Grana Padano is equally good on pasta, or alternatively you can substitute a good, mature cheddar.

MOZZARELLA
Premium mozzarella, a cow's milk cheese, is always fresh and kept in a liquid bath, has a creamy centre, and tastes of fresh milk with a little tang. Buffalo milk mozzarella, made from the milk of water buffalos, is a highly prized speciality of the area around Naples. Never buy the rubbery blocks of mozzarella, as the cheese bears little resemblance to the real thing.

PECORINO
Pecorino means sheep's milk cheese; it is made in almost every area of Italy. The cheese ranges from hard, salty, sharp, and mainly used for grating (Pecorino Romano, from Rome, is the best known); to nutty and round in flavour and ideal for eating or grating; to fresh and creamy with an earthy undertaste. Locatelli Romano is a brand of Pecorino Romano and not a different cheese. If Pecorino Romano is not available, try an aged sheep's milk cheese. For a nutty medium-aged sheep's milk cheese with some tang, use fontinella. For a fresh, creamy and tangy pecorino, try very mild domestic goat's milk cheese or Italian ricotta salata.

RICOTTA
Most supermarket ricotta lacks the creamy, sweet and silken quality of fine ricotta. Seek out the freshest possible in good delicatessens, or blend 4 tbsp whipping cream into each 250g (8oz) of supermarket ricotta. Sheep's milk ricotta is highly prized, but difficult to find.

RICOTTA SALATA
Imported from central and southern Italy, this salted fresh sheep's milk ricotta is pressed into cylinders about 18 x 10cm (7 x 4in). It tastes clean, sweet-salty and fresh. Use wherever a lively, refreshing quality is needed. Shave or crumble it over pastas and salads or serve it as an antipasto with roast peppers, olives and rustic bread. You can find ricotta salata in some supermarkets and delicatessens. Feta is a good substitute.

MASCARPONE
This intensely rich fresh cow's milk cheese from northern Italy, resembling very thick whipped cream, is found in many stores these days. It can be imitated by stirring together until smooth 250g (8oz) cream cheese, softened, 125ml (4floz) sour cream and 4 tbsp double cream.

Clockwise from top (opposite): Parmigiano-Reggiano, ricotta salata, Pecorino Romano, ricotta, mozzarella, mascarpone, Pecorino Toscano, fontina. "Homemade" mascarpone, above.

RULES FOR EATING PASTA

- Italians eat pasta without accompaniment either as a first course or a main course. They claim that it is so complex in the mouth that it would be compromised if served as a side dish or with an accompaniment.

- Allow 60g (2oz) dried pasta for a first course (90g/3oz fresh) and at least 125g (4oz) dried pasta for a main course (155g/5oz fresh). 500g (1lb) dried pasta (625g/1¼ lb fresh) serves 6 to 8 as a first course and 4 or 5 as a main course.

- Keep pasta hot by serving it in bowls rather than on flat plates. Warm the bowls beforehand in a 100°C (200°F) Gas ¼ oven.

- Most Italians favour eating pasta with a fork, not a fork and spoon. Eat long pasta gracefully by taking up only a few strands with your fork; brace the fork on the inside rim of your pasta bowl, and twirl until all the strands are wrapped around the fork.

- Knives and pasta do not go together. Long pastas are twirled onto the fork; baked or filled pastas are cut with the side of a dinner fork.

- Holding a napkin over your chest to shield your shirt from pasta sauce gone astray is in perfectly good form. Tucking the napkin into a collar is more of a family style of eating.

- Buy cheese for pasta in chunks, not pre-grated. It loses moisture once it has been grated. Grate just before sprinkling over the dish.

- Italians rarely use cheese with seafood pasta, adamantly claiming that cheese overwhelms the delicate flavours of many fish and other seafoods.

- Leftover pasta can be very good when reheated with a little olive oil or butter in a frying pan over medium heat. Some cooks add a bit of water to guard against scorching or sticking. This is family snacking and never the way pasta is first served.

PASTA AND NUTRITION

Pasta is made from wheat. From a nutritional standpoint, it joins other grain foods as the foundation of healthy diets and is the basis of many traditional cuisines. Many people believe that pasta is fattening and try to avoid eating it. This is a misunderstanding, as pasta is composed mainly of starch and protein, both relatively low in calories compared to fat. Most pasta dishes contain sauce, cheese, meat or vegetables that balance the starch and prevent unusual fluctuation in blood sugar levels. Sauces do contribute calories. People who are concerned about calories should keep the portion sizes within reasonable limits, use tomato rather than cream sauces, and add just small amounts of meat or cheese.

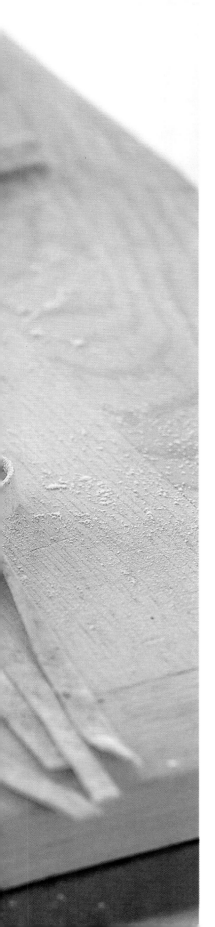

ABOUT
FRESH
PASTA

*F*resh pasta is generally made with unbleached plain flour rather than the durum semolina flour used for dried pasta. Whole eggs, egg whites, and water and/or wine are used to moisten the flour, and sometimes seasonings, salt and olive oil are also added. Colourful flavoured pastas, 24, are also simply made by including puréed vegetables such as spinach or a scattering of chopped fresh herbs. Whatever type of fresh pasta you choose to make, it should rest for at least an hour after cutting and before cooking. For leftovers, see Drying Fresh Pasta, 29.

Herb Pasta, 24

Fresh Egg Pasta

About 875g (1¾ lb)

As the ingredients list that follows makes clear, fresh egg pasta is simplicity itself – just flour and eggs. All the more reason why the ingredients you use should be of the best quality. You have the option of using egg whites in place of whole eggs for fat-free, cholesterol-free fresh pasta. Salt enhances the flavour; so does extra-virgin olive oil, which also gives the pasta an even more supple texture.
Pour onto a clean counter, shape into a mound, and make a well in the centre of:

550g (18oz) unbleached plain flour, preferably stone ground organic

Add to the well in the flour:

5 large eggs or 7 large egg whites
1 tsp salt (optional)
1 tsp extra-virgin olive oil (optional)

Beat the eggs lightly with a fork, drawing in some flour as you go, until the eggs are mixed and slightly thickened. Using the fingertips of one hand, gradually incorporate the flour into the eggs and blend everything into a smooth, not too stiff dough. If the dough feels too dry and crumbly, add water as needed. Alternatively, process the ingredients in a food processor just until blended, 15 to 20 seconds, being careful not to overheat the dough. Knead the dough until satiny and very elastic, about 10 minutes. Divide the dough into 4 pieces and wrap the pieces loosely in cling film or cover with an inverted bowl. If you have time, let the dough rest for 30 minutes before rolling it out.

WHOLEMEAL PASTA

About 875g (1¾ lb)

Serve this pasta with a robust sauce.
Prepare *Fresh Egg Pasta, above,* substituting 155-235g (5-7½oz) wholemeal flour for the same amount of plain flour. This dough may need a little more liquid.

SPINACH PASTA

About 875g (1¾ lb)

Spinach turns this pasta a pale green.
Cook 315g (10oz) fresh spinach, trimmed, washed and dried, or thaw 185g (6oz) frozen spinach. Squeeze the spinach dry and chop it very fine. Prepare *Fresh Egg Pasta, above,* decreasing the eggs to 2. Add the spinach to the flour with the eggs.

HERB PASTA

About 875g (1¾ lb)

This pasta is flecked with green. Choose your favourite herb.
Prepare *Fresh Egg Pasta, above,* adding 60g (2oz) chopped strong fresh herbs (sage, rosemary, thyme, oregano or marjoram) or 185g (6oz) chopped mild fresh herbs (basil, chives, parsley, or spring onions) to the flour with the eggs.

ESPECIALLY STRONG PASTA

About 875g (1¾ lb)

Use this recipe for moist fillings and light-bodied ribbon noodles.
Prepare *Fresh Egg Pasta, above,* substituting 125ml (4floz) cool water or white wine for 3 of the eggs.

Egg Quality, Grades and Sizes

The quality of an egg is largely a matter of how old it is; the best eggs are the freshest. Age is not the only determining factor, however. The shell naturally protects an egg, and if it is cracked or damaged, the contents will deteriorate rapidly; eggs with cracked, damaged or dirty shells should not be used. Also important are the variables of temperature (eggs should be stored at less than 4°C/40°F), humidity (the ideal range is 70 to 80 percent), and handling (which means prompt and frequent gathering, along with washing and oiling of the shell by the producer). A week-old egg, properly stored, can be fresher than an egg left at room temperature for just one day. Check the date or freshness code required on a box from a British Egg Information Service approved packing station. Try to buy eggs from a refrigerated case rather than a room-temperature display.

A fresh egg has a round, shapely, high-standing yolk surrounded by a thick, translucent white. The chalazae cords that anchor the yolk in place should be clearly evident. As an egg ages, the yolk flattens out. The white, cloudy when extremely fresh, becomes clear, thin and runny. If you are unsure of the age of your eggs, just before using them, place them in a bowl of cold water. Those that float – a sign that the egg inside has shrunk through extended moisture loss – are not usable. You can also break an egg into a clean bowl and smell it. An old or stale egg will smell like damp grass and will taint any delicate or pure egg dishes.

Most eggs sold in the supermarkets are graded and labelled A-C, and come in four sizes (very large, large, medium and small). Grade A eggs should be clean and undamaged and conform to rigid specifications in terms of the size of the air space and the texture of the white and yolk. Only packing centres, which have been subject to special registrations by the British Egg Information Council, are authorised to pack Grade A eggs. Grade B eggs have less rigorous specifications, and Grade C eggs are those that do not fit the specifications for A or B. These grades have no bearing on size or freshness.

The most common egg size sold today is medium, and our recipes, unless they state otherwise, use medium eggs.

Rolling Out Fresh Pasta

The key to light, resilient pasta is gently stretching and pulling the sheet of dough as you roll it thinner and thinner. Whether working with a rolling pin (opposite) or a hand-cranked pasta machine (below) work with only a quarter of the pasta at a time, leaving the rest loosely covered. If the pasta becomes too elastic and hard to work with, let it rest a while, covered, so its gluten strands will relax.

Avoid automatic pasta machines that mix and then extrude finished pasta – the results are inferior to pasta rolled by hand or through a hand-cranked pasta machine.

HOW TO WORK PASTA BY MACHINE

1 Set the machine's rollers at the widest setting. Lightly flour 1 of the 4 pieces of dough. Pass the dough through the rollers three times.

2 Fold the dough over onto itself each time. Sprinkle flour on the dough any time it threatens to stick. Guide the dough as it comes out of the rollers with the palm of your hand, held flat to protect the dough from being punctured by your fingers.

3 Set the rollers one notch closer together and repeat the process another two or three times. Stop flouring the dough when it is no longer sticky. The dough should go from lumpy and even holey to a satiny sheet.

As this happens, begin to stretch the dough gently as it emerges from the rollers. Continue to notch the rollers closer together and roll the pasta through them until you reach the desired thickness, 1mm (1/32 in) for ribbon pastas, such as fettuccine, tagliatelle, maltagliati and others; the dough must be paper thin for filled shapes.

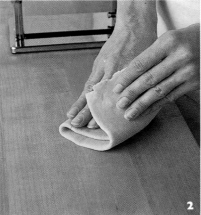

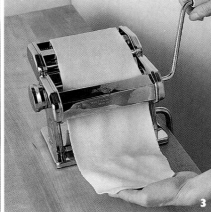

HOW TO WORK PASTA BY HAND

1 Lightly flour a large surface and use a rolling pin to roll out 1 piece of the dough, repeatedly turning it a quarter turn as the circle grows.

2 When the pasta is about 3mm (⅛ in) thick, pick it up and wind it around the rolling pin a quarter of the way towards you.

3 At the same time, stretch the dough gently sideways by running your palms over it from the pin's centre outwards.

4 Unroll the dough, turn the round a quarter of a turn, and repeat this winding and sideways stretching three more times.

5 Then stretch the dough from the centre by winding a third of it back onto the pin and gently pushing the pin away from you; keep the rest of the dough in place with the palm of your other hand.

6 Turn the dough a quarter turn and repeat until the entire circle of dough is stretched and the dough reaches the desired thickness. For ribbon pastas, such as fettuccine, tagliatelle, maltagliati, and others, the dough should be about 1mm (¹⁄₃₂ in) thick, thin enough to detect the outline of your hand through it. For filled pasta, the sheets should be thinner still – sheer enough to see your hand clearly through it.

Pasta Shapes

Ribbons and unfilled shapes are cut pasta sheets that have partially dried. Before cutting, let the pasta sheet dry on a clean counter until it feels leathery but not at all stiff, about 20 minutes. Use a sharp knife or pizza cutter to cut it into ribbons, strips or squares. Dry the cut pasta further in an airy place – on large flat baskets covered with tea towels, or separate the strands and drape them over dowels or broom handles – until it is no longer moist and sticky. Semi-dry ribbon pastas can be dusted with semolina flour to prevent sticking, wrapped in coils and set on racks or in baskets for drying. If not using the pasta immediately, dry it thoroughly and store in sealed containers. Do not freeze. Although it is best cooked the same day, dried homemade pasta is very good indeed several days later.

HOW TO MAKE FARFALLE

Farfalle *is the Italian word for butterfly. Pinched in the middle as it is, this cut pasta is named for the creature it is thought to resemble – a butterfly. You can use either a chef's knife or a zigzag cutter to cut the rectangular pieces of pasta dough you will need to make this shape. That decision aside, the process could not be simpler.*

1 Cut the sheets of rolled-out pasta into rectangles about 4 × 2.5cm (1½ × 1in) in size.

2 Pinch each rectangle firmly together at the centre to make a butterfly shape. Let dry before cooking so that the pasta holds its shape when added to the pot of boiling water. Farfalle have more dough at the centre and less dough at the ends. Test the pasta often during cooking to ensure it is neither under- nor overcooked.

CUTTING NOODLES

Sheets of fresh egg pasta are easily cut into a variety of shapes and sizes. For narrower ribbons such as fettuccine or tagliatelle, you can cut them by passing a sheet of rolled-out pasta through the cutting rollers of a hand-cranked pasta machine. Any size or shape may also be cut by hand. For ribbons, roll up a sheet of fresh pasta like a swiss roll and, with a sharp knife, cut across the roll to make noodles of the desired width. Rectangles for shapes such as lasagne may be formed by spreading a sheet of pasta on a cutting board and using a pastry wheel.

- Fettuccine: Cut long strands a little wider than 3mm (⅛ in).
- Lasagne: Cut into rectangles about 20 x 10cm (8 x 4in).
- Lasagnette: Cut into 2.5cm (1in) wide strips.
- Pappardelle: Cut ribbons 2cm (¾ in) wide.
- Tagliatelle: Cut ribbons just under 1cm (⅜ in) wide.
- Trenette: Roll out the dough a little thicker than usual and cut strands 5mm (¼ in) wide.

DRYING FRESH PASTA

Unfilled fresh pasta is best not frozen but allowed to dry at room temperature. Until it is dried, make sure the pieces do not touch. Hang the fresh pasta from a rack or spread it on shallow baskets, or when it is partially dry, sprinkle it with semolina flour and roll into loose coils. The dried pasta will keep for several days; it may crack if held longer, but the flavour will not be changed.

ABOUT
TOMATO
SAUCES
FOR PASTA

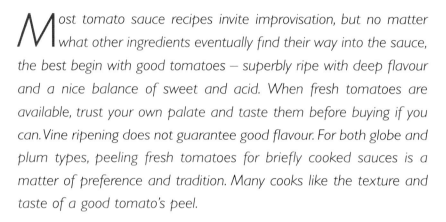

*M*ost tomato sauce recipes invite improvisation, but no matter what other ingredients eventually find their way into the sauce, the best begin with good tomatoes – superbly ripe with deep flavour and a nice balance of sweet and acid. When fresh tomatoes are available, trust your own palate and taste them before buying if you can. Vine ripening does not guarantee good flavour. For both globe and plum types, peeling fresh tomatoes for briefly cooked sauces is a matter of preference and tradition. Many cooks like the texture and taste of a good tomato's peel.

When flavourful fresh tomatoes are unavailable, choose good-quality tinned whole tomatoes for best flavour. Tins of crushed and puréed tomatoes often contain generous amounts of inferior tomato purée, which can impart a heavy, metallic taste.

The faster a tomato sauce is cooked, the fresher and brighter its flavour; hence, we prefer wide frying pans that let liquids evaporate quickly rather than saucepans that slow down the process. When generous amounts of aromatic vegetables and other seasonings enter a recipe, a longer simmer (20 to 30 minutes) in a saucepan encourages flavours to unfold and meld. Likewise, meat-based tomato sauces often are cooked longer still.

Classic Neapolitan Tomato Sauce II, 42

Tomatoes

Whether you enjoy it cooked in a quickly sautéed or slowly simmered pasta sauce, or raw in a salad to accompany a pasta meal, there's nothing like the taste of a home-grown tomato. Unfortunately, that rare flavour can only be enjoyed in the tomato growing season, from midsummer to the first frost.

Tomatoes come in many sizes but only two basic shapes: round and oval. Cherry tomatoes are usually the first round tomatoes in season. Their skins are relatively tough, but their flesh is sweet and juicy. They may be red, gold, orange or yellow-green. Currant tomatoes, imported from South America, are the size and shape of currants and the closest things to wild tomatoes that most of us will ever taste. Their flavour is ultrasweet, especially the yellow ones.

Most standard-sized round toma-toes are as juicy as cherry tomatoes. Several sizes found in most markets offer an even greater variety, and home gardens can provide the best selection of all. Salad tomatoes are small to medium in size and tend to be moderately juicy. Large beefsteak tomatoes (one of the largest varieties) are usually served sliced. In season, they are meaty, rich and juicy, not to mention dark and deep in colour. Also look for so-called heritage or heirloom varieties of tomatoes, seasonal treats that come in a rainbow of colours and even patterns, with delightfully distinctive flavours to match.

Oval-shaped tomatoes, also known as plum tomatoes, are small to medium in size. They are particu-larly valued in cooking because their flesh is thick, meaty, and almost dry. These are the tomatoes favoured by Italian cooks for their pasta sauces.

Sometimes they are called Roma tomatoes (the best-known variety) and they are the ones used to make classic tomato purée. They contribute a tangy-sweet flavour not just to pasta sauces but to soups, gratins, stews or any other cooked tomato dish. You can also use plum tomatoes raw in uncooked sauces, in salads, and whenever juiced tomatoes are called for – just skip the juicing step called for in a particular recipe.

Whatever the type, most tomatoes raised for mass commerce are picked green and continue to develop their red colour off the vine. But since sugars cannot increase in a fruit after picking, their flavour will not improve with ripening. The finest commercial tomatoes will be labelled "vine-ripened". Although usually harvested not fully matured, they will have spent more time on the vine and will have begun to show their colour at the time of picking.

In Britain, most tomatoes are grown under glass. This extends the natural season (from July to October) so tomatoes can be harvested between March and December. Under glasshouse conditions, the environment is computer-controlled, but bumble bees are used for pollination and pests are biologically controlled by natural predators.

When shopping for any tomatoes, select firm, bright specimens that feel heavy for their size. Scarring around the stem end is harmless. Any stems or leaves still attached should look moist and fresh. If the tomato smells like a tomato, grab it. Homegrown tomatoes should be picked when they are fragrant. Whether you grow tomatoes in season yourself or buy peak-of-season tomatoes from local growers, eat them the same day they are picked if possible. If using tomatoes outside their peak season, try to buy the tomatoes a few days in advance of using. Set them on a tray by a window, making sure they are not touching, and leave for a few days to ripen. Never store tomatoes in the refrigerator, as chilling gives the flesh a pappy texture.

Tomatoes have great affinities with butter, olive and nut oils, cheese in any form, onions, garlic any type of basil, oregano, sage, thyme, dill, parsley, rosemary, coriander, rice, seafood, avocados, cucumbers, peppers, aubergine, okra, beans, squash, eggs, bread, potatoes, walnuts, olives and capers. Of course, they are also the basis for some of the most delicious and easy to make of all pasta sauces. Allow 125 to 250g (4 to 8oz) per serving.

HOW TO PEEL, SEED, AND JUICE TOMATOES

1 Cut a small X in the bottom of the tomatoes – do not cut the flesh. Ease the tomatoes one by one into a pot of boiling water. Leave ripe tomatoes in for about 15 seconds, barely ripe tomatoes in for twice as long. Lift them out with a sieve and drop into a bowl of iced water to stop the cooking.

2 Pull off the skin with the tip of the knife. If the skin sticks, return the tomato to the boiling water for another 10 seconds. If the dish can use a touch of smoky flavour, hold the tomato on a long-handled fork over a gas burner, turning it until the skin splits. Do not plunge in water, but peel the tomato as directed above.

3 To seed and juice a tomato, cut it crosswise in half (between the top and bottom). Squeeze each half gently, cut side down, over a sieve set in a bowl to catch the juice, which you can add to pasta sauces. Now run the tip of a finger into each of the cavities and flick out the mass of seeds into the sieve.

Twenty-Minute Tomato Sauce

Enough for 500g (1lb) pasta

Heat in a medium saucepan over medium heat:

2 tbsp extra-virgin olive oil

Add:

1 medium onion, chopped

2 medium carrots, peeled and chopped

2 cloves garlic, finely chopped

Cook, stirring, until softened, about 5 minutes. Stir in:

Two 400g (14oz) tins whole tomatoes, with juice, broken into pieces

1 tbsp dried basil

1-2 tsp dried oregano

Simmer, uncovered, until the sauce is thickened, about 10 minutes. Remove to a food processor and pulse until smooth. Return to the saucepan and stir in:

1-2 tsp sugar

½ -1 tsp crushed chilli flakes

Salt and ground black pepper to taste

Heat through, about 5 minutes.

Simplest Italian Tomato Sauce Marinara

Enough for 500g (1lb) pasta

Marinara sauce consists simply of oil and garlic with chopped tomatoes added; its many variations include puttanesca (with olives and capers) and red clam sauce.

Bring to a simmer in a large saucepan over medium-low heat:

1kg (2lb) ripe tomatoes, peeled, if desired, seeded, and coarsely chopped, or two 400g (14oz) tins whole tomatoes, with juice, crushed between your fingers as you add them to the pan

80ml (3floz) extra-virgin olive oil

3 cloves garlic, halved

6 sprigs fresh basil

6 sprigs fresh parsley

Simmer, uncovered, until the sauce is thickened, about 10 minutes. Pass through a food mill and season with:

Salt and ground black pepper to taste

SHOP-BOUGHT SAUCES

When shopping for prepared sauces, look for those with the fewest preservatives. Simple tricks to boost the flavour of a shop-bought sauce are:

- A drizzle of good olive oil and a sprinkling of ground black pepper
- A handful of fresh mushrooms, sliced and sautéed
- A few good-quality stoned olives and drained capers
- A tin of tuna, drained
- A mixture of fresh herbs, chopped

ITALIAN HERBS

Pungent and aromatic, basil is a perfect complement to tomatoes, and blends well with garlic and thyme. Perhaps this is why it is traditional in Italian and other Mediterranean cooking. Peppery with a hint of mint and clove, basil's flavour becomes more intense during cooking.

Oregano and marjoram are closely related and easily confused. Both are members of the mint family. Oregano is earthier, and its leaves are larger and darker. Leaves are medium green and somewhat heart shaped, from 5mm to 4cm (¼ to 1½ in) long. Of the many varieties, Greek oregano and sweet marjoram set the standard. Sweet marjoram is a summer herb – spicy, sweet, and intense yet light.

Parsley is not only a flavourful herb, but also valuable as an agent in cooking for blending the flavours of other herbs. It is an excellent addition to savoury dishes, but does not work well with sweets. Flat-leaf parsley is the most flavourful of the parsley varieties, and the curly leaf variety is primarily used for garnish. Fresh parsley is claimed by some to destroy the scent of garlic and onion on your breath.

USING AND STORING HERBS

When cooking with herbs, snip them with scissors or chop by hand. Most fresh herbs are perishable, and careful storage is crucial. Store bunches in the refrigerator, their stems immersed in water like a bouquet of flowers. Pack loose leaves and flowers, and rhizomes such as ginger, in perforated plastic bags in the vegetable drawer of the refrigerator. If there is excess moisture in the leaves or tubers, before packing, pat them fairly dry, then crush a dry paper towel at the bottom of the bag and place the leaves on top. A little moisture helps keep plant parts fresh, but keep in mind that too much promotes decay.

It is important to remember that strengths in leaves vary, but the general rule when substituting dried herbs for fresh is to use a generous ¼ teaspoon ground or 1 teaspoon crumbled dried leaves for every tablespoon of the fresh herb finely chopped.

Italian Tomato Sauce

Enough for 500g (1lb) pasta

This classic tomato sauce and any of its variations can be kept in the refrigerator for up to 4 days or frozen for up to 3 months.

Heat in a large frying pan over medium heat:

2-3 tbsp extra-virgin olive oil

Add:

5 tbsp finely chopped fresh parsley
1 medium onion, finely chopped
1 small carrot, peeled and finely chopped
1 celery stalk with leaves, finely chopped

Cook, stirring, until the onions are golden brown, about 5 minutes. Add:

2 cloves garlic, finely chopped

15g (½oz) packed fresh basil leaves, chopped, or 1 sprig each fresh rosemary, sage and thyme

Cook, stirring, for about 30 seconds. Stir in:

1.25kg (2½ lb) ripe tomatoes, peeled, if desired, seeded, and coarsely chopped, or three 400g (14oz) tins whole tomatoes, with juice, crushed between your fingers as you add them to the pan
1 tbsp tomato purée (optional)
Salt and ground black pepper to taste

Simmer, uncovered, until the sauce is thickened, about 10 minutes. Remove the herb sprigs.

SUN-DRIED TOMATO SAUCE

Enough for 500g (1lb) pasta

Put 45g (1½oz) sun-dried tomatoes (not in oil) in a small bowl, add boiling water to cover, and let soak until softened, about 20 minutes. Drain well and finely chop. Prepare *Italian Tomato Sauce, above left,* decreasing the fresh tomatoes to 1kg (2lb) or the tinned tomatoes to 1kg (2lb), and adding the sun-dried tomatoes with the garlic.

PIQUANT TOMATO SAUCE

Enough for 500g (1lb) pasta

Prepare *Italian Tomato Sauce, above left,* substituting 1 whole dried red chilli pepper (a bit less if you prefer the sauce less fiery) for the carrots and celery and decreasing the basil to just a few leaves. Remove the chilli pepper before serving.

Puttanesca Sauce

Enough for 500g (1lb) pasta

Spicy, savoury and exciting, Puttanesca, or Streetwalker's, Sauce (opposite) is ready to toss with pasta in minutes.

Heat in a large frying pan over medium heat:

60ml (2floz) extra-virgin olive oil

Add:

2 large cloves garlic, finely chopped
1 dried red chilli pepper

Cook, stirring and crushing the pepper with the back of a spoon, just until the garlic is pale golden, about 30 seconds. Stir in:

185g (6oz) oil-cured black olives, such as Gaeta, stoned and coarsely chopped
6 anchovy fillets, soaked in water to cover for 5 minutes and drained

½ tsp dried oregano

Cook for about 30 seconds, then stir in:

750g (1½ lb) ripe tomatoes, peeled, if desired, seeded, and chopped, or two 400g (14oz) tins whole tomatoes, with juice, crushed between your fingers as you add them to the pan

Simmer, uncovered, until the sauce is thickened, about 5 minutes. Stir in:

3 tbsp chopped fresh parsley
2 tbsp drained capers

Season with:

Salt and ground black pepper to taste

Fresh Tomato Sauce

Enough for 500g (1lb) pasta

Summer's best. Make this easy sauce when you can get juicy, ripe tomatoes.

Drain in a colander for 20 minutes:

5 large ripe tomatoes, seeded and finely diced

Remove to a large bowl and stir in:

15g (½oz) fresh basil leaves, finely chopped

3 tbsp extra-virgin olive oil

2 cloves garlic, finely chopped

Salt and ground black pepper to taste

Let stand for at least 30 minutes. Serve the sauce at room temperature. If serving over hot pasta, sprinkle each portion with:

1-2 tsp balsamic vinegar

FRESH TOMATO SAUCE WITH MOZZARELLA

Enough for 500g (1lb) pasta

Prepare *Fresh Tomato Sauce, left.* Add 250g (8oz) fresh mozzarella cheese, cut into small cubes, to the hot pasta and toss before adding the tomato sauce.

FRESH TOMATO SAUCE WITH BLACK OLIVES

Enough for 500g (1lb) pasta

Prepare *Fresh Tomato Sauce, left.* Stir in 90g (3oz) stoned black or Kalamata olives to the sauce.

FRESH TOMATO SAUCE WITH FRESH OREGANO OR PARSLEY

Enough for 500g (1lb) pasta

If your garden or local market is filled with herbs, feel free to mix and match. Prepare *Fresh Tomato Sauce, left,* substituting fresh oregano or parsley for the basil.

FRESH TOMATO SAUCE WITH HOT CHILLI PEPPER

Enough for 500g (1lb) pasta

Prepare *Fresh Tomato Sauce, left.* Stir in 1 small fresh chilli pepper, seeded and finely chopped.

ITALIAN AND GREEK OLIVES

Gaeta olives from Italy are brownish black, smoothly soft, with a nutty, almost earthy, flavour. Other Italian olives include the mellow tan-coloured Calabrese, the salty and firm black Lugano, and the quite piquant and tart, brown-black Liguria. For a special treat try Sicilian green olives; they are tart and meaty.

The famous Kalamata olives from Greece are purple-black or maroon with a slender oval shape, soft texture, and rich flavour. Royal olives are cured with oil and vinegar and so are slightly chewy, with a similar flavour to Kalamatas but a more reddish hue.

Buy olives that are uniform in colour and free of surface blemishes and white spots. Keep loose olives in the refrigerator for several weeks; tinned or bottled olives can be kept unopened on the shelf for up to two years and when opened should be refrigerated as loose olives.

Classic Neapolitan Tomato Sauce I

Enough for 500g (1lb) pasta

This is the sauce Italian grandmothers had simmering on their stoves for half a day.

Heat in a large flameproof casserole over medium-high heat:

2 tbsp olive oil, preferably extra-virgin

Add:

750g (1½ lb) boneless loin of pork or beef steak, in 1 piece

Brown on all sides. Add:

250g (8oz) diced onions
125g (4oz) prosciutto or pancetta, chopped
2 cloves garlic, finely chopped

Reduce the heat to medium and cook, stirring the vegetables and prosciutto around the piece of meat, until the onions are softened, about 10 minutes. Stir in:

250ml (8floz) water

Cook until the water is almost evaporated and has made a little bit of sauce around the onions, 20 to 25 minutes. Stir in:

1.75kg (3½ lb) ripe tomatoes, peeled, if desired, seeded, and chopped, or four 400g (14oz) tins whole tomatoes, with juice, crushed between your fingers as you add them to the pan
250ml (8floz) red wine
60ml (2floz) tomato purée
1 sprig fresh basil or oregano, or 1 tsp dried

Bring to a boil, reduce the heat and simmer, uncovered, stirring often, turning the meat halfway through the cooking time, until the meat offers no resistance when pierced with the tip of a sharp knife and is fall-apart tender, 3 to 4 hours. Remove the meat and set aside to cool. Cook down the sauce if it is not thick, and season with:

Salt and ground black pepper to taste

Place in a medium frying pan over medium heat:

500g (1lb) coarse herbed sausages

As soon as the sausages have released some of their fat, increase the heat to medium-high to help with the browning. Cut the sausages into 5mm (¼ in) thick slices and stir into the sauce. Finely chop the reserved piece of meat or process in a food processor until finely chopped but not a paste. If chopping by hand, remove to a bowl. Add to either the bowl or processor:

2 large eggs
75g (2½ oz) fresh breadcrumbs
15g (½ oz) chopped fresh parsley
75g (2½ oz) grated Parmesan
½ tsp salt
Ground black pepper to taste

Stir together well or process just to mix, then shape into 2.5cm (1in) meatballs. Heat in a large frying pan over medium-high heat:

2 tbsp olive oil

Brown the meatballs, about 1 minute each side, adding more oil as needed. Stir into the sauce.

PROSCIUTTO AND PANCETTA

Prosciutto means "ham" in Italian, and it is exquisite ham. Hogs are specially raised on a diet of chestnuts or, in the Parma region, on the whey from the local Parmesan cheese production. The hind legs are dry-cured and air-dried for a minimum of ten months, giving the meat a firm, dry quality with a pronounced flavour. Prosciutto needs no cooking and, in fact, can become dry and tough if cooked. It is often added at the end of cooking for flavour and is commonly served sliced paper-thin with sliced melons or figs or used sparingly to season soups and stews. Look for prosciutto di Parma imported from Italy and avoid domestic varieties of unsmoked, salt-cured ham, which do not compare. It should be stored well-wrapped in the refrigerator for no more than three days.

Pancetta is the Italian version of bacon from the pork belly (*pancia*). The most commonly found pancetta is sold in packages of small cubes or sold by weight in slab form by the butcher. Pancetta is not smoked, so it is more moist and has a mellower flavour than smoked bacon. The incomparable spicy-sweet taste of pancetta comes from the mixture of salt, black pepper, and spices used to cure the pork. Pancetta is commonly used as a flavouring for stews and braises by rendering the fat and using it to cook other ingredients. It is also a fine savoury addition to stuffings of all sorts. Pancetta can be stored in the freezer for up to three months. Unsmoked streaky bacon can be used as a substitution.

Classic Neapolitan Tomato Sauce II

Enough for 500g (1lb) pasta

An American-style Italian dish unsurpassed in its ability to please family and friends. Of course, the sauce and meatballs are traditionally served with spaghetti, but other strands or ribbons such as linguine or tagliatelle may also be used. The meatballs and sauce also make a fine dish served on their own without pasta or tucked into crusty rolls to make robust Italian meatball sandwiches.

With the machine running, drop through the feed tube of a food processor:

1 clove garlic, peeled
15g (½ oz) fresh parsley leaves
125g (4oz) Parmesan or Asiago cheese, cut into coarse chunks

Process until the cheese is finely grated. Add:

1 medium onion, halved

Process until finely grated. Remove to a large bowl. Add and blend well:

500g (1lb) lean minced beef, or 250g (8oz) lean minced beef and 250g (8oz) minced turkey
45g (1½ oz) fresh breadcrumbs
1 large egg, lightly beaten
3 tbsp dry red wine
2 tbsp tomato purée
½ tsp salt
⅛ tsp ground black pepper

Shape into about fourteen 5-7.5cm (2-3in) meatballs.
Dredge lightly with:

Plain flour

Heat in a large frying pan over medium-high heat:

2-3 tbsp extra-virgin olive oil

Add the meatballs and brown on the bottom. Turn and sprinkle with:

1 medium onion, finely chopped

Brown the meatballs on all sides. Pour off the fat in the pan and add:

1 clove garlic, finely chopped
¼ tsp dried oregano

Stir in:

Two 400g (14oz) tins whole tomatoes, with juice, crushed between your fingers as you add them to the pan

Bring to a simmer and cover the pan. Reduce the heat and simmer gently, stirring occasionally, until the meatballs are cooked and the sauce is thickened, about 30 minutes.

ITALIAN-STYLE MEATBALLS

Prepare the meat mixture for *Classic Neapolitan Tomato Sauce II, left.* Shape into meatballs 1-2cm (½ - ¾ in) in diameter. Brown in olive oil, then simmer in a little white wine and *Chicken Stock, 17,* for about 20 minutes. Serve hot as an antipasto or a main course without the tomato sauce.

Bolognese Sauce (Ragù Bolognese)

Enough for 500g (1lb) pasta

This famous sauce from the northern Italian city of Bologna has many subtle tastes that come together beautifully through long, gentle simmering followed by reheating the next day. The milk in the sauce, a surprising but traditional addition, adds a sweet, mellow flavour.

Heat in a large saucepan over medium-low heat:

3 tbsp extra-virgin olive oil
30g (1oz) pancetta, finely chopped (optional)

Cook, stirring, until the pancetta releases its fat but is not browned, about 8 minutes. Increase the heat to medium and add:

1 large carrot, peeled and chopped
2 small celery stalks, chopped
½ medium onion, chopped

Cook, stirring, until the onions are translucent, about 5 minutes. Add and brown:

625g (1¼ lb) coarsely minced beef rump steak or very lean minced chuck

Stir in:

180ml (6floz) Chicken Stock, 17, or Beef Stock, 17

160ml (5floz) dry white wine
2 tbsp tomato purée

Reduce the heat to low and simmer gently, partially covered and skimming occasionally, until the sauce is the consistency of a thick soup, about 2 hours. From time to time as the sauce simmers, add, 2 tbsp at a time:

375ml (12floz) whole milk

Let cool, cover, and refrigerate for up to 24 hours. Skim the fat off the top before reheating.

Chicken Ragù

Enough for 500g (1lb) pasta

Pappardelle is traditionally served with a sauce made from game, but chicken makes a delicious substitute in this richly flavoured sauce. To freeze the sauce, do not add the mushrooms. Sauté and blend in the mushrooms shortly before serving.

Heat in a large flameproof casserole over low heat:

3 tbsp extra-virgin olive oil

Add:

60g (2oz) salt pork, diced
1 medium onion, finely chopped
1 carrot, peeled and finely chopped
1 celery stalk, finely chopped

Cook, stirring occasionally, until the vegetables are softened and beginning to brown, about 8 minutes. Add to the casserole:

500g (1lb) boneless chicken thighs, diced

Season with:

Salt and ground black pepper to taste

Increase the heat to medium and brown on all sides, about 5 minutes. Stir in and cook until almost evaporated:

125ml (4floz) dry white wine

Stir in:

250ml (8floz) Chicken Stock, 17
Two 400g (14oz) tins whole plum tomatoes, drained and chopped

Reduce the heat to low and simmer, partially covered, until the chicken is tender, about 1½ hours. Sprinkle with:

6 fresh sage leaves, chopped
Salt and ground black pepper to taste

Melt in a medium frying pan over medium heat:

3 tbsp butter

Add and cook, stirring, until browned:

250g (8oz) mushrooms, wiped clean and halved
Salt and ground black pepper to taste

Add the mushrooms to the sauce.

SALT PORK

From the fatty part of the belly, knuckle, or even shoulder comes this heavily salted unsmoked product prized for its fat, which is commonly rendered for cooking in Central Europe and in America. A chunk of salt pork added to a pasta sauce during cooking lends a savoury richness to the entire dish.

Since the advent of refrigeration, salted meats are today subjected to much weaker brining than formerly. You may, however, find that, depending on the brand, the salt pork is still too salty for your taste. If that is the case, soak the salt pork before use to cut down on its saltiness. The method for doing so is known as *à blanc* – blanching the meat in simmering water just until its colour changes. Bacon can be substituted without soaking first.

Penne with Vodka

8 first-course servings; 4 main-course servings

Here is a modern Italian pasta dish that is elegant enough to begin a formal dinner. Use a good-quality vodka to achieve the finest flavour.

Melt or heat in a large frying pan over medium heat:

45g (1½oz) butter or 3 tbsp olive oil

Add:

1 onion, finely chopped

Cook, stirring, until softened, about 5 minutes. Add:

2 large cloves garlic, finely chopped

Cook, stirring, until just starting to colour, about 1 minute. Stir in:

Two 400g (14oz) tins whole plum tomatoes, lightly drained and chopped by hand or in a food processor
60ml (2floz) vodka
¼ tsp crushed chilli flakes

Simmer briskly for 10 minutes. Stir in:

125ml (4floz) double cream

Heat through. Stir in:

12 fresh basil leaves, chopped (optional)

Salt and ground black pepper to taste

Meanwhile, bring to a rolling boil in a large pot:

6 litres (10 pints) water
2 tbsp salt

Add and cook until tender but firm:

500g (1lb) penne

Drain and remove to a large serving bowl. Toss with the sauce and serve very hot. Grated cheese is not usually served with this sauce.

Bow Ties with Spicy Chicken Bits and Broccoli

8 first-course servings; 4 main-course servings

A quick and zesty supper or first course. This dish is also an excellent way to use up leftover pieces of boneless chicken.

Bring to a rolling boil in a large pot:

6 litres (10 pints) water

2 tbsp salt

Add and cook until tender but firm:

625g (1¼ lb) fresh farfalle, or 500g (1lb) dried

Meanwhile, combine in a large bowl:

4 boneless, skinless chicken breasts, cut into bite-sized pieces

185g (6oz) broccoli pieces (florets and chopped stems)

2 tsp grated lemon zest

¼ tsp cayenne pepper

¼ tsp ground black pepper

Pinch of salt

Heat in a large frying pan over high heat:

3 tbsp olive oil, preferably extra-virgin

Add the chicken mixture and cook, stirring, until browned, about 5 minutes. Stir in:

125ml (4floz) dry white wine

125ml (4floz) tomato purée

185g (6oz) stoned black olives

2 tbsp drained nonpareil capers

Simmer, uncovered, for 5 minutes. Drain the pasta and toss it with the sauce. Serve immediately with:

Grated pecorino cheese

CAPERS

These are the preserved buds of a white flower on a spiny Mediterranean shrub. Freshly picked, the buds are startlingly bitter, reminiscent of raw artichoke hearts. Once cured in salt or brine, their flavour mellows without losing its citrus-like tartness. The smallest caper buds are called nonpareil. Large, fully formed caper berries, with their stems still attached, are also available and are quite dramatic in appearance, especially when used to garnish gin and vodka martinis. The one essential ingredient in tapenade is the caper – *tapano* in Provençal. Capers are far better packed under salt but are usually found in brine. Always drain and rinse capers before using, however they are packed. Chopped gherkins can be used instead of capers in some dishes.

Pasta and Beans (Pasta e Fagioli)

8 first-course servings; 4 main-course servings

More a soup than a stew, pasta e fagioli *is a beloved dish in Italy.*

Heat in a large saucepan over medium heat:

2 tbsp extra-virgin olive oil

Add:

1 medium onion, finely chopped

1 small carrot, peeled and finely chopped

1 medium celery stalk with leaves, finely chopped

2 tbsp finely chopped fresh parsley

Cook, stirring, until the onions are golden brown, about 10 minutes. Stir in:

2 large cloves garlic, finely chopped

Cook for 1 minute. Add:

400g (14oz) tin whole tomatoes, with juice, crushed between your fingers as you add them to the pan

Boil, stirring, until thickened, about 3 minutes. Stir in:

400g (14oz) tin cannellini, butter beans or pinto beans, rinsed and drained

500ml (16floz) Chicken Stock, 17

155g (5oz) green beans, cut into 2.5cm (1in) pieces

185g (6oz) frozen small broad beans

Return to a boil. Stir in:

185g (6oz) frisée, escarole, curly endive or Swiss chard, washed, dried and cut into 2.5cm (1in) pieces

Partially cover and simmer for 5 minutes. Stir in:

60g (2oz) macaroni

Salt to taste

Cook until the macaroni is tender but firm, about 15 minutes. Thin, if needed, with additional:

Stock

Season with:

Ground black pepper to taste

Just before serving, stir in:

30g (1oz) grated pecorino cheese

Ladle into bowls and serve immediately, passing additional:

Grated pecorino cheese

WHITE BEANS

Butter beans are about twice the size of navy (or pea) beans; these two are the most commonly available white beans and are excellent baked or in soups. Cannellini are often called white kidney beans, but the two are different though related; white kidney beans are like red kidney beans in size and texture, while cannellini are slimmer and creamier when cooked. All of these white beans, part of the kidney bean clan, can be used interchangeably, with consideration given to the size of the bean if relevant to the recipe. Flageolets are white to pale green immature kidney beans. Both their colour and delicate flavour place them firmly in the white bean family, but they taste slightly more like fresh beans and hold their shape very well when cooked. Their firmness makes them a good choice for salads.

ABOUT **OTHER SAUCES** FOR PASTA

*T*he simplest pasta sauce consists of little more than olive oil with the addition of garlic. Aglio e olio (merely garlic and oil) is a southern Italian classic. The uncomplicated vegetable sauces of southern Italy are made by adding courgettes, cauliflower, sprouting broccoli, peppers, beans and other local vegetables to the olive oil base; other typical additions include anchovies, red chilli peppers and fresh herbs. Pesto Sauce, 52, the classic sauce of Genoa, is made by mixing fresh basil, cheese and pine nuts with that region's fragrant olive oil and garlic.

Because most of us are familiar with southern Italian cooking, we think of Italy as a land of tomato sauce. In parts of northern Italy where butter prevails, you are likely to come across egg pasta tossed with nothing more than the local butter and maybe a little cream and grated Parmesan, the local cheese. Many of the country's meat-based sauces contain very little tomato, even in the south. In Tuscany, beef sauces are flavoured with olive oil and sometimes red wine. Rome is famous for its lamb ragù. All these long-cooked sauces develop complex flavours from a reduction of wine and meat stocks.

Porcini and Red Wine Sauce, 53

Spaghetti with Garlic and Oil (Aglio e Olio)

8 first-course servings; 4 main-course servings

A simple sauce of olive oil and garlic is one of the purest ways of enjoying good-quality spaghetti or other skinny ribbon-shaped pasta. A little bit of the pasta cooking water helps the sautéed garlic cling to the pasta.

Bring to a rolling boil in a large pot:

6 litres (10 pints) water
2 tbsp salt

Add and cook until tender but firm:

500g (1lb) spaghetti

Meanwhile, heat in a large frying pan over medium heat:

3 tbsp extra-virgin olive oil

Add:

3 large cloves garlic, thinly sliced
1 dried red chilli (optional)

Cook, stirring, until the garlic is pale golden, about 2 minutes. Remove the chilli. Drain the spaghetti, reserving 125ml (4floz) of the cooking water. Add the cooking water and hot pasta to the garlic mixture and toss to combine. Add:

**Salt and ground black pepper
to taste**

Serve hot. No cheese should be served with this dish.

Straw and Hay (Paglia e Fieno)

8 first-course servings; 4 main-course servings

This quick, but luxuriously good dish gets its name from the mix of green and yellow fettuccine.

Bring to a rolling boil in a large pot:

6 litres (10 pints) water
2 tbsp salt

Add and cook until tender but firm:

**375g (12oz) fresh spinach
fettuccine or 250g (8oz) dried**
**375g (12oz) fresh egg fettuccine,
or 250g (8oz) dried**

Meanwhile, heat in a large frying pan over medium heat:

15g (½ oz) butter

Add and cook for 1 minute:

60g (2oz) prosciutto, chopped

Add and boil for 2 minutes:

250ml (8floz) double cream

Stir in and cook 2 minutes more:

315g (10oz) frozen peas

Drain the pasta and add it to the frying pan along with:

60g (2oz) prosciutto, chopped
**75g (2½oz) freshly grated
Parmesan cheese**
**Salt and ground black pepper
to taste**

Serve immediately.

GARLIC

Fresh garlic comes to market in summer, but this member of the onion (and thus of the lily) family is available all year round. Choose plump, firm heads of cloves with tight, papery skins that may be white, purplish or tinged with red. Store away from light at room temperature. Avoid using cloves with brown spots or green sprouts – they are past their prime.

The bunches of green garlic you may find at the farmers' market are garlic at the immature stage – just as spring onions are the immature stage of cooking onions. The flavour of the immature bulbs and tender green leaves is exquisite. Prepare and store it as you would spring onions, but use as you would garlic.

Elephant garlic is not true garlic but a form of leek. Its white- or purple-skinned cloves are the size of brazil nuts, and their flavour is mild enough not to require cooking. Peel the cloves as you would an onion and use as you would garlic.

EXTRA-VIRGIN OLIVE OILS

These oils are the premium ones that are pressed and processed without heat or solvents. Colour is no indication of quality and ranges from gold to deep green, depending upon where and with what olives the oil is made. Clouded, unfiltered oils are prized by many for their sometimes fuller flavour. Lamentably the words "extra-virgin" on the bottle do not guarantee good-tasting oil. If at all possible, sample before buying any quantity. Use extra-virgin oil for seasoning, salads and cooking.

Fettuccine Alfredo

8 first-course servings; 4 main-course servings

Traditionally prepared tableside in restaurants, this simple, classic dish is extraordinary when made with fresh egg fettuccine, double cream, and authentic Parmigiano-Reggiano cheese.

Bring to a rolling boil in a large pot:
6 litres (10 pints) water
2 tbsp salt

Add and cook until tender but firm:
625g (1¼ lb) fresh fettuccine, or 500g (1lb) dried

Melt in a large frying pan over medium heat:
125g (4oz) unsalted butter

Drain the pasta and add it to the frying pan along with:

250ml (8floz) double cream
75g (2½oz) freshly grated Parmesan cheese
Salt and ground black pepper to taste

Toss over low heat until the pasta is well coated. Serve immediately.

Fettuccine with Butter and Cheese

8 first-course servings; 4 main-course servings

Use freshly grated Parmigiano-Reggiano for the best flavour in this pasta dish, which takes moments to make.

Bring to a rolling boil in a large pot:
6 litres (10 pints) water
2 tbsp salt

Add and cook until tender but firm:
625g (1¼ lb) fresh fettuccine or tagliatelle, or 500g (1lb) dried

Drain and toss the hot pasta with:
125g (4oz) unsalted butter, softened, or 5 tbsp extra-virgin olive oil
125g (4oz) grated Parmesan cheese

Season with:
Salt and ground black pepper to taste

Serve immediately.

> **LESS BUTTERY BUTTER AND CHEESE SAUCE**
>
> Boil 375ml (12floz) *Chicken Stock, 17,* until reduced by half. Stir in 45g (1½oz) unsalted butter. Meanwhile, prepare the pasta for *Fettuccine with Butter and Cheese, left.* Toss the stock mixture with the hot pasta and Parmesan cheese. Season with salt and ground black pepper to taste.

Pesto Sauce

Enough for 500g (1lb) pasta

This classic sauce from Genoa needs to be made with fresh basil. Pesto (left), is traditionally tossed with trenette, a flat ribbon pasta similar to linguine but fresh. Sometimes green beans and sliced potatoes are cooked along with the pasta in the same water, making the dish more robust. If freezing, add the nuts and cheese after thawing.

Process to a rough paste in a food processor:

75g (2½ oz) fresh basil leaves
75g (2½ oz) pine nuts
2 medium cloves garlic, peeled
60g (2oz) grated Parmesan cheese

With the machine running, slowly pour through the feed tube:

125ml (4floz) extra-virgin olive oil

If the sauce seems dry (it should be a thick paste), add a little more olive oil. Season with:

**Salt and ground black pepper
  to taste**

Use immediately or store in a covered glass jar in the refrigerator for up to 1 week.

Red Pesto Sauce

Enough for 500g (1lb) pasta

Sun-dried tomatoes may have originated in Italy, but British and American cooks have invented uses barely conceived of in Italy. Reserve 125ml (4floz) of the pasta cooking water to stir into the pesto so it will toss more easily with the pasta. Otherwise, just add hot water to thin it to the desired consistency.

Combine in a small saucepan with enough water to cover:

**5 tbsp chopped drained water-
  packed sun-dried tomatoes**
1 clove garlic, peeled
6 fresh basil leaves

Bring to a boil, remove from the heat, and let stand for 20 minutes. With the machine running, drop through the feed tube of a food processor:

1 large clove garlic, peeled
30g (1oz) fresh basil leaves

60ml (2floz) extra-virgin olive oil
**30g (1oz) freshly grated Parmesan
  cheese**

Drain the tomato mixture, add to the processor, and finely chop. Season with:

**Salt and ground black pepper
  to taste**

Stir in:

**125ml (4floz) pasta cooking water
  or hot water**

Porcini and Red Wine Sauce

Enough for 500g (1lb) pasta

A robust and meaty-tasting sauce with little or no meat and the haunting woodsy taste of porcini mushrooms. Soak in hot water to cover until softened, about 20 minutes:

45g (1½ oz) dried porcini mushrooms, thoroughly rinsed

Remove the mushrooms with a slotted spoon and chop. Strain and reserve the soaking liquid. Heat in a large frying pan over medium-high heat:

2 tbsp extra-virgin olive oil

60g (2oz) pancetta, finely chopped (optional)

Add:

½ medium onion, chopped

Zest of ½ lemon, cut into very thin strips

4 fresh or dried sage leaves

Cook, stirring, until the onions are softened. Add the porcini along with:

250g (8oz) button mushrooms, wiped clean and thinly sliced

Increase the heat to high and cook,

stirring, until the mushrooms are golden brown. Stir in:

1 clove garlic, finely chopped

Stir in the porcini soaking liquid. Simmer briskly until the liquid is reduced to a glaze. Stir in and reduce again to a glaze:

250ml (8floz) dry red wine

Stir in:

250ml (8floz) Chicken Stock, 17

Season with:

Salt and ground black pepper to taste

MUSHROOMS

Porcini, also called cèpes or boletes, look like very large button mushrooms with thick stalks and reddish caps. They are among the tastiest of wild mushrooms, something to enjoy simply. When fresh porcini are not available, look for dried (above). They need to be rinsed well and soaked before cooking. So flavourful are dried porcini mushrooms that the water in which they soak becomes well flavoured, too. It needs to be strained before use.

White button mushrooms are rounded, plump, creamy and mild. Select only those with closed caps. If they are very small, use them whole. Larger ones may be halved or sliced. To clean fresh mushrooms, wipe them gently with a damp paper towel.

Fettuccine with Fresh Herbs

8 first-course servings; 4 main-course servings

Bring to a rolling boil in a large pot:

6 litres (10 pints) water

2 tbsp salt

Add and cook until tender but firm:

625g (1¼ lb) fresh fettuccine, or 500g (1lb) dried

Meanwhile, rub a warmed serving bowl with:

1 clove garlic, halved

Combine in the bowl:

3-4 tbsp extra-virgin olive oil

30g (1oz) fresh basil leaves, finely chopped

30g (1oz) finely snipped fresh chives

4 tbsp fresh oregano or marjoram leaves, finely chopped

90g (3oz) grated Parmesan cheese, or 280g (9oz) crumbled ricotta

Salt and ground black pepper to taste

Drain the pasta and toss it with the herb mixture. Serve hot.

Fettuccine Primavera

8 first-course servings; 4 main-course servings

Any seasonal vegetable can be added or substituted in this easy but elegant sauce. Just make sure that whatever vegetables you use are cut into small pieces of about the same size so the sauce has a uniform look. Add each at the appropriate stage of preparation so that all are done uniformly tender. You might try sugar snap peas, artichokes, green beans, spring onions or courgettes.

Bring to a rolling boil in a large pot:

6 litres (10 pints) water
2 tbsp salt

Add and cook for 1 minute:

6 asparagus, tough ends trimmed, finely diced, tips left whole
1 small bunch broccoli, stemmed and cut into very small florets

Remove the vegetables with a sieve and rinse under cold water to stop the cooking. Reserve the vegetable cooking water. Heat in a large frying pan over medium heat:

2 tbsp olive oil
45g (1½oz) butter

Add:

1 large onion, finely diced
2 carrots, peeled and finely diced

Cook, stirring, until softened, about 5 minutes. Add the blanched asparagus and broccoli along with:

125g (4oz) fresh or thawed frozen peas

Salt and ground black pepper to taste

Cook, stirring, until all the vegetables are tender. Return the vegetable cooking water to a boil. Add and cook until tender but firm:

500g (1lb) fresh fettuccine, or 375g (12oz) dried

Stir into the vegetables:

250ml (8floz) double cream

Simmer over medium heat while the pasta is cooking. Drain the pasta and add it to the sauce along with:

12 fresh basil leaves, chopped
60g (2oz) grated Parmesan cheese

Toss to coat over low heat. Serve very hot.

Penne with Prawns and Fresh Chilli Peppers

8 first-course servings; 4 main-course servings

Ready in the time it takes to boil the pasta. The orange zest adds a pleasant zing to this spicy dish.

Bring to a rolling boil in a large pot:

6 litres (10 pints) water

2 tbsp salt

Add and cook until tender but firm:

500g (1lb) penne

Meanwhile, heat in a large frying pan over medium heat:

60ml (2 fl oz) olive oil

Add and cook until the garlic turns golden:

8 cloves garlic, chopped

Zest of 1 orange, chopped

1-2 mild to hot fresh chilli peppers, seeded and diced

Add:

500g (1lb) prawns, peeled, deveined and diced

Cook, stirring, until the prawns are barely firm, about 3 minutes. Remove 125ml (4 fl oz) of the pasta cooking water and stir it into the prawns. Drain the pasta and toss it with the sauce. Season with:

Salt and ground black pepper to taste

Serve hot.

Spinach Fettuccine with Smoked Salmon and Asparagus

8 first-course servings; 4 main-course servings

Smoked salmon, although not an Italian ingredient, is now often found in pasta sauces in both Italy and elsewhere. A little of the rich, very flavourful sauce (opposite) goes a long way.

Bring to a rolling boil in a large pot:

6 litres (10 pints) water

2 tbsp salt

Add and cook until tender but firm, 1 to 4 minutes depending on their thickness:

500g (1lb) fresh asparagus, tough ends trimmed, cut into 2.5cm (1in) pieces

Scoop out the asparagus with a sieve and rinse under cold water to stop the cooking and preserve the bright green colour. Return the cooking liquid to a rolling boil. Add and cook until tender but firm:

625g (1¼ lb) fresh spinach fettuccine, or 500g (1lb) dried

Meanwhile, melt in a large frying pan over medium heat:

45g (1½oz) unsalted butter

Add the asparagus and cook, stirring, just to coat with butter, about

1 minute. Stir in and heat through:

250ml (8floz) double cream

Grated zest of 1 lemon

Drain the pasta and add it to the pan along with:

125g (4oz) smoked salmon, cut into thin strips, or cooked fresh salmon, cut into small pieces

4 tbsp snipped fresh chives

4 tbsp chopped fresh parsley

Salt and ground black pepper to taste

Toss to combine and serve immediately.

Tinned Tuna Sauce

Enough for 500g (1lb) pasta

Slow-cooked garlic gives this sauce its deep flavours. If you can, use tuna packed in olive oil. If serving with pasta, reserve 125ml (4floz) of the pasta cooking water to stir into the sauce.

Heat in a large frying pan over medium-low heat:

60ml (2floz) extra-virgin olive oil

Add:

2 tbsp chopped fresh parsley

8 large cloves garlic, halved

Cook, stirring, until the garlic is

softened, about 20 minutes. Do not let the garlic darken further than golden, or it will be bitter. Stir in:

3 anchovy fillets, rinsed, patted dry and chopped

185g (6oz) oil-cured black olives, stoned and coarsely chopped

125ml (4floz) pasta cooking water or hot water

½ tsp fennel seeds, crushed (optional)

Generous pinch of crushed chilli flakes

Cook for 1 minute, remove from the heat, and stir in:

185g (6oz) tin tuna, drained and flaked

1 tbsp drained capers (optional)

1 tbsp chopped fresh parsley

Salt and ground black pepper to taste

Bucatini with Seafood Sauce

8 first-course servings; 4 main-course servings

Choose a variety of seafood for this sauce (opposite) including firm-fleshed fish with lots of flavour, such as bluefish, bass and swordfish, as well as a variety of shellfish, such as prawns, diced squid or octopus, scallops, crabmeat, mussels and clams. Avoid sand in the sauce by precooking any mussels or clams. Strain the shellfish cooking liquid into the sauce, adding the cooked shellfish just long enough to heat it through.

Heat in a large frying pan over medium heat:

3 tbsp olive oil

Add and cook just until pale blond:

3 cloves garlic, sliced paper thin

Using a slotted spoon, transfer the garlic to a small bowl. Increase the heat to medium-high and add (wait to add cooked mussels and clams at the end):

1 kg (2 lb) assorted seafood, such as firm-fleshed fish fillets and shellfish, cut into 2.5 cm (1 in) pieces

Cook, stirring, just until the fish are opaque and barely firm to the touch. Using a slotted spoon, transfer to a bowl. Add to the pan:

160 ml (5 fl oz) dry white wine
Several fresh basil leaves

Simmer, scraping up any browned bits on the bottom of the pan, until the wine has evaporated. Stir in:

1 kg (2 lb) ripe tomatoes, peeled, seeded and chopped
Cooking liquid from clams and/or mussels if using

Simmer, uncovered, until the sauce is thickened, about 10 minutes. Add the seafood to the sauce, along with precooked clams or mussels if using. Simmer until heated through. Season with:

Salt and ground black pepper to taste

Meanwhile, bring to a rolling boil in a large pot:

6 litres (10 pints) water
2 tbsp salt

Add and cook until tender but firm:

500 g (1 lb) bucatini

Drain the pasta and toss it with the sauce. Add the reserved garlic and toss to combine. Drizzle over:

Extra-virgin olive oil

Serve hot without cheese.

HARD-SHELL CLAMS

Hard-shell clams vary more in size and colour than in shape. They all have firm, sometimes tough, meat with excellent, briny flavour. And all are essentially free of grit. Venus are the smallest of hard-shell clams, preferably considerably under 5 cm (2 in) across. They are good eaten raw and excellent in quick-cooking sauces. Larger clams can measure from 5-10 cm (2-4 in) across. They too are excellent for cooking.

Linguine with White Clam Sauce

8 first-course servings; 4 main-course servings

Made for years up and down Italy's coast, and a favourite in Italian restaurants in the United States. In some areas a little tomato is added, in others chilli pepper or herbs and white wine, but the constant is the freshest of clams.

Boil in a large frying pan for 5 minutes:

500 ml (16 fl oz) water
60 ml (2 fl oz) dry white wine
½ tsp dried oregano
5 parsley stems
1 bay leaf
Pinch of crushed chilli flakes (optional)

Add:

2 kg (4 lb) small clams (such as Venus), scrubbed

Simmer, covered, until the shells open. Remove the clams from the broth, discarding any unopened ones, and shell them, reserving any juice. Strain the broth and reserve. Wipe out the pan. Cook, stirring, for a few minutes:

2 tbsp olive oil
1 large clove garlic, finely chopped
2 tbsp finely chopped fresh parsley

Meanwhile, bring to a rolling boil in a large pot:

6 litres (10 pints) water
2 tbsp salt

Add and cook until tender but firm:

500 g (1 lb) linguine

Drain the pasta. Add the pasta, reserved clams with juice and broth to the pan. Toss with:

2 tbsp chopped fresh parsley

Serve immediately.

Spaghetti alla Carbonara

8 first-course servings; 4 main-course servings

Italian bacon (pancetta) and cheese-flavoured eggs tossed with spaghetti, this is another Roman tradition made in no time and an old favourite with Americans as Sunday brunch fare. Legend has it that the Italian name means "spaghetti in the coal miners' style", referring to the humble workers who reportedly originated the dish. Pancetta is not smoked, so it is more moist and has a mellower flavour than bacon.

Heat in a large frying pan over medium-high heat:

1 tbsp extra-virgin olive oil

Add and cook, stirring, until crisp:

185g (6oz) pancetta or bacon, finely diced

Pour off all but 3 tbsp fat from the pan. Meanwhile, bring to a rolling boil in a large pot:

6 litres (10 pints) water
2 tbsp salt

Add and cook until tender but firm:

500g (1lb) spaghetti

Reserve 80ml (3floz) of the pasta cooking water and combine it with:

4 large eggs, lightly beaten
30g (1oz) grated pecorino cheese

Drain the pasta and add it while very hot to the pan. Add the egg mixture and toss over medium heat until the eggs are firm. Season with:

Ground black pepper to taste

Serve hot, passing separately:

90-180g (3-6oz) grated pecorino cheese

Orecchiette with Sausage and Sprouting Broccoli

8 first-course servings; 4 main-course servings

Sprouting broccoli is a pleasantly bitter vegetable. If it is not available, broccoli can be substituted. Use 500-750g (1-1½ lb) broccoli, stems coarsely chopped.

Heat in a large frying pan over medium heat:

60ml (2floz) olive oil, preferably extra-virgin

Add:

4 coarse Italian sausages (about 500g/1lb), casings removed

Cook, breaking the meat up with a spoon, until nicely browned, about 5 minutes. Stir in:

3 large cloves garlic, finely chopped
¼ tsp crushed chilli flakes

Cook for 1 minute more. Stir in:

1 large bunch sprouting broccoli, washed, dried and coarsely chopped

Cover and cook just until tender, about 5 minutes. Meanwhile, bring to a rolling boil in a large pot:

6 litres (10 pints) water
2 tbsp salt

Add and cook until tender but firm:

500g (1lb) orecchiette or other short dried pasta

Drain the pasta, leaving some water clinging to the noodles, and add it to the pan over low heat. Toss to coat and combine, then remove to a large serving bowl (opposite). Season with:

Salt and ground black pepper to taste

Sprinkle with:

30g (1oz) grated pecorino cheese

Serve immediately, passing additional:

Grated cheese

ABOUT
FILLED &
BAKED
PASTAS

*W*hether filled and boiled or layered and baked, pasta can be as light and ethereal as Crespelle, 79, or as hearty and sustaining as Lasagne Bolognese, 72, with a whole world of recipes in between. Many of these, such as Individual Baked Shells with Red Pepper Purée, 76, *ravioli and tortellini, come to the table from Italian traditions, but filled pasta comes from other cuisines, too.* Vareniki, 69, *for example, are of Russian descent and* Pastitsio, 75, *comes from Greece.*

Many baked pasta dishes function as casseroles – capable of serving a crowd or holding up well if and when served as leftovers. For all these dishes, both the sauce and the filling can be made a day ahead.

Roast Red Pepper and Herb Goat's Cheese Lasagne, 70

Making Filled Pasta by Hand

For the pasta, make *Fresh Egg Pasta*, 24, or *Especially Strong Pasta*, 24, if the filling is moist. The fresh pasta sheets must be filled and shaped immediately after they are rolled out, while they are still moist. Roll the pasta thin enough to see your hand through it and keep the sheets moist by covering them with cling film as you work. Please read *Freezing Filled Pasta*, below.

FREEZING FILLED PASTA

Pastas with moist fillings or stuffed with fresh or creamy cheese do not freeze well. Pastas stuffed with firm meat fillings or others that are essentially dry will freeze well. To freeze pasta, line a large baking tray with aluminium foil. Spread out the filled pasta so that the pieces do not touch. Freeze overnight. Gently drop the pieces into heavy freezer bags and seal, leaving some air in the bag to protect the pasta from being crushed. Freeze for up to 3 months.

HOW TO MAKE RAVIOLI

Ravioli can be filled with cheese or meat.

1 Cover half a sheet of freshly rolled pasta with mounds of ½ tsp each of the chosen filling spaced 2.5cm (1in) apart. Dip your finger in water and run it around the filling.

2 Fold over the unfilled half of the pasta sheet, taking care to cover each mound so that no air is trapped.

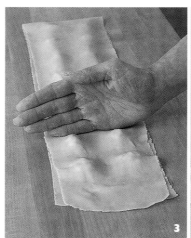

3 With the side of your hand, press firmly to seal the sheets of dough around the filling.

4 Use a zigzag cutter to cut the sheet into squares or rectangles, checking that each piece is well sealed.

HOW TO MAKE TORTELLINI AND CAPPELLETTI

Tortellini are traditionally filled with meat, and are wonderful as a first course, as a main dish, used in pasta salads or added to soups. Cappelletti are filled with cheeses or other fillings, depending on the region. For filled pasta, keep in mind that it is best to have the filling prepared before making the pasta, since you need to fill and shape the pasta while it is still moist.

1 To create these little doughnuts of filled pasta, cut freshly rolled sheets of pasta into 4.5cm (1¾ in) rounds.

2 Place ¼ tsp filling in the centre of each round.

3 Fold each round in half and seal the edges.

4 Bring the tails of the half circle together, overlapping them, and twist one over the other.

Cooking Filled and Baked Pastas

For each 500g (1lb) of pasta, bring 8 litres (13 pints) salted water to a rolling boil. Add the pasta, reduce the heat and simmer, uncovered, so as not to break apart the delicate shapes. Most filled pastas will float to the surface when they are done. Be careful not to overcrowd the pot; if you must, cook the pasta in batches. To cook frozen filled pasta, simply slip the still-frozen pieces into the boiling water and cook for an extra minute or two.

Baked pasta dishes range from traditional Italian lasagne with sheets of homemade pasta to macaroni and cheese. They have long been popular dishes to serve to large numbers – entertaining or family gatherings. For all these dishes, both the sauce and the filling can be made a day ahead. Since the pasta is cooked twice in these recipes, boil it only long enough to be pliable and barely tender.

Some pasta shapes, such as lasagne, manicotti and cannelloni, are cooked before they are filled and baked in a casserole. These pastas can be found on the following pages. Many of the fillings that follow can be used interchangeably for filled and baked pastas.

Simple Cheese Filling

Enough to fill 100 to 150 pieces

Use this filling in a variety of filled and stuffed pastas. It is also wonderful as a stuffing for baked vegetables, such as mushroom caps or pepper halves.

Stir together in a large bowl:

375g (12oz) good-quality ricotta cheese

125g (4oz) grated Parmesan, kasseri or fontinella cheese

125g (4oz) shredded fresh mozzarella cheese

¼ medium onion, finely chopped

6 spring onions, finely chopped

4 tbsp fresh oregano leaves, finely chopped

4 tbsp fresh basil leaves, finely chopped (optional)

1 clove garlic, finely chopped

Salt and ground black pepper to taste

Taste and adjust the seasonings, then add:

1 large egg, lightly beaten

Store, covered, in the refrigerator for up to 24 hours.

Vegetable Cheese Filling

Enough for 500g (1lb) large pasta

Perfect for manicotti, this filling also works for large shells, ravioli, lasagne or ziti.

Soak in warm water to cover for 20 minutes:

1 tbsp dried currants (optional)

Drain and set aside. Meanwhile, bring to a rolling boil in a large pot:

250ml (8floz) water

Add and simmer, uncovered, until softened:

250g (8oz) fresh spinach or 375g (12oz) Swiss chard, trimmed, or 185g (6oz) frisée, escarole or radicchio, washed and dried

Drain, squeeze dry and finely chop.

Heat in a medium frying pan over medium-high heat:

1 tbsp extra-virgin olive oil

Add and cook until browned:

60g (2oz) finely chopped onion

30g (1oz) pancetta or prosciutto, finely chopped (optional)

Stir in:

1 small clove garlic, finely chopped

Cook for 30 seconds (be careful not to burn the garlic). Stir in the greens and cook for 2 minutes. Let cool, then blend with the drained currants and:

250g (8oz) ricotta cheese

75g (2½ oz) grated Parmesan cheese

1½ tbsp pine nuts, toasted

Freshly grated or ground nutmeg to taste

Salt and ground black pepper to taste

Taste and adjust the seasonings, then stir in:

1 large egg, lightly beaten

This filling will keep, covered and refrigerated, for up to 24 hours.

Meat Filling

Enough to fill 100 to 150 pieces

Use this blend of sautéed meats, cheese and prosciutto to fill ravioli, tortellini or cappelletti, or spread it over lasagne. You can omit the pork if you wish, and add instead 185g (6oz) more of poultry.

Have ready:

155g (5oz) grated Parmesan cheese

Melt or heat in a medium frying pan over medium-high heat:

15-30g (½-1oz) butter or 1-2 tbsp extra-virgin olive oil

Add:

125-155g (4-5oz) boneless, skinless turkey or chicken breasts, thinly sliced

One 2.5cm (1in) thick pork loin chop (250-280g/8-9oz), boned, trimmed, and thinly sliced

2 tbsp finely chopped onion

Salt and ground black pepper to taste

Cook, stirring often, until browned and cooked through, 4 to 5 minutes. Stir in:

60ml (2floz) dry white wine

Bring to a boil, scraping up the browned bits on the bottom of the pan. Remove from the heat, let cool and remove to a food processor. Add 90g (3oz) of the cheese along with:

125g (4oz) mortadella

90g (3oz) prosciutto

Pinch of ground nutmeg

Salt and ground black pepper to taste

Process until finely chopped and well blended. (The meats can also be chopped by hand.) Taste and adjust the seasonings. There should be just a hint of nutmeg. Stir in the remaining cheese. At this point, the filling can be covered and refrigerated for up to 2 days.

NUTMEG AND MACE

Two spices come from the brown, oval seed of a fruit resembling an apricot, which grows on a tropical evergreen tree. Wrapped around the shell of the seed is a lacy sheath. A blade of mace is one segment of the lacy covering, called the aril. Scarlet when the fruit is opened, the aril dries to a shade of orange. Mace is sold whole or as a ground spice. Several weeks after harvest, when the kernel has shrunk in its shell, the thin shell is cracked and the kernel removed. This is nutmeg – brown, solid and hard. Nutmeg is best freshly grated but can also be purchased already ground. Nutmeg graters are commonly available. As warm a spice as nutmeg is, mace is more refined and can be used in place of nutmeg.

MORTADELLA

Mortadella, which is cooked (rather than dry-aged) sausage, is a purée of pork stuffed into a natural casing. In the northern Italian city of Bologna, where it has been made for many centuries, it is studded with cracked peppercorns and cubes of creamy fat. Soft in texture and subtle in flavour, some varieties feature pistachios or olives. Mortadella is often included in an *affettato*, a traditional Italian assortment of cured meats. In the vicinity of Bologna, it is often put on the table at the beginning of a meal in irregular cubes, rather than thin slices. These nuggets are then eaten with rustic bread.

Vareniki

4 servings

These slightly sweet Russian cheese dumplings are served with butter and sour cream (opposite).

Have ready:

Fresh Egg Pasta, 24

Combine in a medium bowl:

185g (6oz) cottage or curd cheese, drained

1 large egg, beaten

2 tsp melted butter

2 tsp sugar

½ tsp salt

¼ tsp ground nutmeg

Divide the dough into quarters and roll out one piece at a time, keeping the others covered. Roll into a long, thin sheet, about 2mm (1/16 in) thick, and use a biscuit cutter to cut into 6cm (2½ in) circles. Place about ½ tsp of filling in the centre of each circle, close to form a half circle, and pinch the edges together. If necessary, moisten the edges with a little water to help them stick. Bring to a boil in a large pot:

Water

Salt

Add the dumplings in batches to avoid overcrowding. Reduce the heat and simmer until the dumplings float, about 12 minutes. Carefully remove with a strainer or slotted spoon to a warmed bowl. Pour over:

2 tsp melted butter

Serve hot and pass:

Sour cream

SOUR CREAM

Sour milks and creams play an important part in cooking. The presence of lactic acid gives them a more tender curd, and this in turn makes for a more tender crumb in baking and smoother texture in sauces. Sour cream is made by adding a bacterial culture to cream and incubating it at about 22°C (72°F) until the lactose is converted to at least 0.5 percent lactic acid. The cultured cream is then packaged, chilled and aged for 12 to 48 hours. When cooking with sour cream, remember that excessive heat causes curdling.

Pelmeni

4 servings

These Russian meat dumplings can also be fried in butter (after being boiled) and served with sour cream and dill.

Have ready:

Fresh Egg Pasta, 24

Sauté in a medium frying pan:

1 tbsp rendered chicken fat or olive oil

60g (2oz) chopped onion

2 tbsp chopped parsley

250g (8oz) lean minced beef

Add:

Salt and ground black pepper to taste

Let cool slightly and stir in:

1 egg white, beaten

Divide the dough into quarters and roll out one piece at a time, keeping the others covered. Roll into a long, thin sheet, about 2mm (1/16 in) thick. Cut the sheets into 10cm (4in) squares. Place a tablespoon of the meat filling in the centre of each square. Fold the dough over the filling into a triangular shape. Press the open edges together with a fork to seal them. Moisten the edges with a little water to help them stick. Before cooking allow the dumplings to dry on a flour-dusted towel 30 minutes on each side. Bring to a boil in a large pot:

About 4 litres (6½ pints) Chicken Stock, 17, or Brown Beef Stock, 17

Add the dumplings in batches to avoid overcrowding. Reduce the heat and simmer until al dente, about 8 minutes. Carefully remove with some of the stock to a warmed bowl. Sprinkle with:

1 tbsp fresh chopped parsley

Serve immediately.

DILL

As feathery as fennel, these pungent and slightly tangy, somewhat caraway-flavoured leaves are a wonderful complement to many dishes. Dried, the leaves are sold as dill weed. The leaves are best raw; when cooked, they lose strength. Because each leaf is not much thicker than a thread, the warm green leaves make a handsome garnish. The small, flat, oval seeds bear a fine dill flavour and can be used every way the leaves are used. Butter yellow and borne in inverted umbrellas, the tender flower heads can be used just like the leaves; in fact they are particularly appealing in a jar of pickles. An alternative is caraway.

Roast Red Pepper and Herb Goat's Cheese Lasagne

8 to 10 servings

Have ready:

1½ recipes *Simplest Italian Tomato Sauce Marinara*, 34

6 large red peppers, roasted (opposite), peeled, seeded, and coarsely chopped

60g (2oz) grated Parmesan cheese

Combine in a food processor:

1 clove garlic, chopped

3 spring onions, or ½ small onion, chopped

4 tbsp mixed fresh herbs, such as basil and parsley, or 1 tbsp mixed dried oregano and parsley

Two 315-375g (10-11oz) logs fresh mild goat's cheese

Up to 4 tbsp double cream

Salt and ground black pepper to taste

Process until creamy and smooth. The filling should be easy to spread. If it is too stiff, add:

Up to 180ml (6floz) double cream

Bring to a rolling boil in a large pot:

8 litres (13 pints) water

2 tbsp salt

Add and cook until barely tender:

500g (1lb) fresh lasagne, or 500g (1lb) dried

Preheat the oven to 190°C (375°F) Gas 5. Lightly oil a 33 x 23 x 7.5cm (13 x 9 x 3in) baking or lasagne pan. Spread a thin layer of the tomato sauce over the bottom of the dish. Cover the sauce with a layer of pasta, overlapping the sheets by 1cm (½ in). Spread with one-quarter of the cheese filling and top with one-quarter of the red peppers. Ladle enough tomato sauce to just barely cover the layer and sprinkle with one-quarter of the Parmesan cheese. Repeat the layers 3 more times until all the ingredients are used, finishing with tomato sauce and Parmesan cheese (4 layers total). Cover the dish with foil and bake until bubbly on top, 20 to 30 minutes for fresh pasta, 45 to 50 minutes for dried pasta. Remove the foil for the last 10 to 15 minutes of baking. Remove from the oven and let stand for 10 minutes before serving.

Pesto Vegetable Lasagne

8 to 10 servings

Soak in warm water to cover for 20 minutes:

1 tbsp dried currants

Drain and set aside. Have ready:

1½ recipes *Pesto Sauce*, 52

In a large pot with only the water that clings to the leaves, cook over medium heat until wilted:

625g (1¼ lb) spinach, trimmed and washed

Drain and let cool in a colander, squeeze dry and finely chop. Heat in a medium frying pan over medium-high heat:

2 tbsp olive oil

Stir in and cook until browned:

60g (2oz) chopped onion

Two 3mm (⅛ in) thick pancetta slices, finely chopped (optional)

3 tbsp pine nuts

Add the currants and spinach along with:

1 small clove garlic, finely chopped

Cook, stirring, for about 2 minutes. Let cool, then blend with:

500g (1lb) whole-milk or skimmed milk ricotta cheese

155g (5oz) grated Parmesan cheese

1 large egg

Freshly grated or ground nutmeg to taste

Salt and ground black pepper to taste

Taste and adjust the seasonings. Bring to a rolling boil in a large pot:

8 litres (13 pints) water

2 tbsp salt

Add and cook until barely tender:

500g (1lb) fresh lasagne, or 375g (12oz) dried

Drain and separate the lasagne. Keep in a bowl of iced water.

Preheat the oven to 180°C (350°F) Gas 4. Lightly oil a 2½ litre (4 pint) shallow baking dish or a 33 x 23 x 7.5cm (13 x 9 x 3in) baking or lasagne pan.

Line the bottom of the dish with a single layer of the lasagne. Spread with one-quarter of the cheese mixture. Spread with one-quarter of the pesto. Repeat the layers 3 more times, until all the ingredients are used. Cover with foil. Bake for 35 minutes. Uncover and bake until the pasta is heated through, about 15 minutes more. Let stand for 5 minutes before serving.

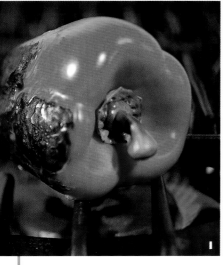

HOW TO ROAST AND PEEL PEPPERS

Roasting provides the best way to remove the skin of peppers. It softens their flesh, tempers the raw taste, and adds a delicious smokiness. Thick-walled peppers can be taken a step further and charred. Thinner-walled peppers are better if blistered but not completely charred, or they will lose flesh when you peel them. Red peppers tend to char faster than green ones, having more sugars in their flesh.

1 *Stove-Roasting Fresh Peppers:* This is the simplest method. Place whole peppers directly in the flames of your gas burner on its highest setting. (If you do not have a gas burner, set the peppers on a grill rack called an asador, one that rests above the burner, or use the grill method.) Keep an eye on the peppers and turn them frequently with tongs, letting the peppers blister or char (do not pierce with a cooking fork, as juices will be lost). Continue until the entire surface is blistered. Many cooks quickly toast, or stove-roast, dried chillies before rehydrating them, to deepen and round out flavours.

2 *Grill-Roasting Fresh Peppers:* Line a grill pan with foil. Place whole peppers on the foil and brush with olive oil. Grill, turning as needed, until blackened on all sides. Alternatively, cut pepper into pieces and place the skin side up on a grill pan. Set the pan 13-15cm (5-6in) under the grill. Grill until the skin starts to blister and brown in places, watching it at every moment. Let the pieces char if you wish the flesh to be well cooked.

Barbecue-Roasting Fresh Peppers: This is the most flavourful method. Set whole peppers on a rack over ash-covered coals, a hot but dying fire. Let them sit in one place until they are blistered or charred, then turn them and repeat until the whole pepper is done.

Griddle- or Pan-Roasting Fresh Peppers: This is for small fresh chillies such as serranos and jalapeños. Heat a dry cast-iron griddle or frying pan over high heat, add the whole peppers and shake them around the frying pan until their skins are charred here and there. These chillies are customarily not peeled after roasting, but they may be.

3 Once they are blistered, lay peppers in a bowl and and be sure to cover with a plate or cling film. Their heat will create steam, which will loosen the skins. Try not to rinse peppers after roasting, for much of the smoky flavour is on the surface. Scrape off the skins with a knife. If the peppers were whole, make a slit down one side, then run the tip of a small serrated knife around the stem underneath the base. Remove the top and the core and seeds that come with it, then scrape away remaining seeds and cut away the membranes. Add any juices in the bottom of the bowl to the dish you are making, or blend them into a vinaigrette dressing for added flavour. Remember that roasting and peeling can be done a day or two in advance. If you do roast peppers in advance, be sure to wrap them airtight and store in the refrigerator.

Lasagne Bolognese

8 to 10 servings

This classic meat lasagne (opposite) is utterly lush. Manage your time by making the béchamel and meat sauces a day or so ahead.

Have ready:

Bolognese Sauce, 43

90g (3oz) grated Parmesan cheese

For the béchamel sauce, melt in a large pot over medium heat:

30g (1oz) butter

Add:

2 tbsp plain flour

Cook, stirring with a wooden spoon, until well blended. Gradually whisk in:

875ml (28floz) milk

Stir in:

1 small onion, halved

½ carrot, peeled and coarsely chopped

4 celery leaves

2 whole cloves

Simmer gently, stirring often, until reduced by one-third, about 15 minutes. Season with:

Freshly grated or ground nutmeg to taste

Salt and ground black pepper to taste

Strain the béchamel sauce into a bowl, pressing against the vegetables with a wooden spoon. Discard the vegetables. Cover the surface of the sauce with cling film. The béchamel sauce can be made ahead and refrigerated for up to 3 days; bring to room temperature before proceeding.

Bring to a rolling boil in a large pot:

8 litres (13 pints) water

2 tbsp salt

Add and cook until barely tender:

625g (1¼ lb) fresh spinach lasagne, or 500g (1lb) dried

Drain and separate the lasagne. Keep in a bowl of iced water. Meanwhile, warm the meat sauce.

Preheat the oven to 180°C (350°F) Gas 4. Lightly oil a 33 x 23 x 7.5cm (13 x 9 x 3in) baking or lasagne pan. Spread a thin layer of meat sauce over the bottom of the dish. Cover with a layer of pasta, overlapping the sheets by 1cm (½ in). Spread a thin layer of béchamel over the lasagne sheets and top with a thin layer of meat sauce. Sprinkle with about 1½ tbsp grated cheese and top with another layer of pasta. Repeat the layers, reserving 80ml (3floz) béchamel and 30g (1oz) cheese to cover the final layer of pasta. Loosely cover with foil and bake for 40 to 50 minutes. Let stand for 10 minutes before serving.

Classic Italian American Lasagne

8 to 10 servings

This was the festive celebration lasagne that leapt from Italian American tables all over the United States. Do not mix the cooked sliced sausage, if using, directly into the sauce. To ensure even distribution, it is layered with the meatballs in this lasagne.

Have ready:

Classic Neapolitan Tomato Sauce I or II, 40, 42

500g (1lb) ricotta cheese

500g (1lb) mozzarella cheese (preferably fresh), thinly sliced or shredded

Preheat the oven to 190°C (375°F) Gas 5. Lightly oil a 33 x 23 x 7.5cm (13 x 9 x 3in) baking or lasagne pan.

Bring to a rolling boil in a large pot:

8 litres (13 pints) water

2 tbsp salt

Add and cook until barely tender:

500g (1lb) fresh lasagne, or 500g (1lb) dried

Drain and separate the lasagne. Arrange a layer of lasagne over the bottom of the pan. Spread with one-third of the ricotta. Scatter one-quarter of the mozzarella over the ricotta and season with:

Salt and ground black pepper to taste

Arrange one-third of the meatballs in the pan, either whole or cut in half, and scatter one-third of the sausage slices over the meatballs. Save 500ml (16floz) of the sauce for the top of the lasagne, then spoon about 250ml (8floz) of sauce over the meat in the pan. Add another layer of lasagne and continue layering the lasagne until all the ingredients are used, giving 4 layers of pasta with 3 layers of filling. Spread the reserved 500ml (16floz) of sauce over the top layer of pasta. Sprinkle the final one-quarter of the mozzarella over the sauce with:

30g (1oz) grated Parmesan cheese

Bake until well browned and bubbly, about 45 minutes. Let stand for 15 minutes before serving.

Pastitsio

8 to 10 servings

Bring to a rolling boil in a large pot:

6 litres (10 pints) water

2 tbsp salt

Add and cook until tender but firm:

500g (1lb) macaroni, penne or other small shaped pasta

Drain and toss with:

1 tbsp extra-virgin olive oil

Meanwhile, for the white sauce, blend in a medium saucepan over low heat:

30g (1oz) butter

3 tbsp plain flour

Cook, stirring constantly, until the mixture stops sizzling, about 3 minutes. Whisk in:

875ml (28floz) milk

½ tsp salt

½ tsp ground white pepper

¼ tsp freshly grated or ground nutmeg

Stir frequently until well blended. The mixture will be very thin. Add:

125ml (4floz) double cream

Simmer, stirring frequently, until thickened, about 5 minutes. Meanwhile, heat in a medium stockpot over medium heat:

½ tbsp olive oil

Add:

1 large onion, chopped

Cook until the onion begins to soften, about 5 minutes. Add:

500g (1lb) minced lamb or beef

1½ tsp finely chopped garlic

Break up the meat with a large spoon and cook until no longer pink. Stir in:

375g (12oz) ripe tomatoes, peeled and chopped, or 400g (14oz) tin whole tomatoes, with juice, coarsely chopped

125ml (4floz) dry red wine

1 tbsp tomato purée

2 tsp ground cinnamon

2 tsp dried marjoram

¼ tsp cayenne pepper

1 tsp salt

½ tsp ground black pepper

Simmer, uncovered, for 15 to 20 minutes. Cool slightly and stir in:

4 tbsp fresh parsley leaves, chopped

Combine the pasta and meat sauce. At this point, the pasta mixture and the white sauce can be covered and refrigerated for a day or two before assembling. To finish, preheat the oven to 190°C (375°F) Gas 5. Grease a 33 x 28cm (13 x 11in) baking dish. Spoon the pasta mixture into the dish. Place the white sauce in a large bowl and mix in:

4 large eggs, beaten

250g (8oz) ricotta cheese

90g (3oz) crumbled feta cheese

Pour the white sauce over the pasta. Sprinkle with:

60g (2oz) grated mature Cheddar or Parmesan cheese

At this point, the casserole can be covered and refrigerated up to 1 day. Bake the pastitsio until set and golden (opposite), 35 to 40 minutes. Let cool slightly before cutting.

Johnny Marzetti Spaghetti Pie

6 to 8 servings

This casserole was made famous at Marzetti's restaurant in Columbus, Ohio. In a 5-6 litre (8-10 pint) flameproof casserole, brown over medium heat until the beef loses most of its pink colour, about 8 minutes:

750g (1½ lb) ground beef chuck

1 large onion, chopped

1 green pepper, chopped

2 cloves garlic, finely chopped

Add:

Two 400g (14oz) tins Italian tomatoes, with juice, chopped

375g (12oz) jar passata

1 tsp dried oregano

1 bay leaf

Salt and ground black pepper to taste

Bring to a boil, reduce the heat to medium-low and simmer, stirring frequently, about 20 minutes. Preheat the oven to 180°C (350°F) Gas 4. Bring to a rolling boil in a large pot:

6 litres (13 pints) water

2 tbsp salt

Add and cook until tender but firm:

500g (1lb) spaghetti, ziti or other dried pasta

Drain well and add to the sauce along with:

90g (3oz) grated mature Cheddar cheese

Mix well and top with:

90g (3oz) fresh breadcrumbs, lightly toasted

90g (3oz) grated mature Cheddar cheese

Bake until the top is lightly browned and the casserole is bubbling, about 30 minutes. Let stand for 5 minutes before serving.

Individual Baked Shells with Red Pepper Purée

6 to 8 first course servings

Preheat the oven to 260°C (500°F) Gas 9. Bring a medium pot of water to a boil. Add and cook for 8 minutes:

2 coarse, spicy Italian sausages

Remove and discard the casings and coarsely chop the sausages. Meanwhile, purée in a blender:

4 medium red peppers, roasted, 71, peeled, and seeded

You should have about 250ml (8floz) purée. In a large bowl, combine the sausage and red pepper purée with:

90g (3oz) chopped tinned tomatoes
500ml (16floz) double cream
45g (1½oz) grated pecorino cheese
60g (2oz) coarsely grated fontina cheese
2 tbsp ricotta cheese
½ tsp salt

Bring to a rolling boil in a large pot:

5 litres (8 pints) water
2 tbsp salt

Add and cook for 4 minutes:

500g (1lb) pasta shells

Drain the pasta, add to the ingredients in the bowl, and toss to combine. Divide the pasta mixture among 6 to 8 individual gratin dishes, about 375-500ml (12-16floz) in capacity. Dot with:

60g (2oz) unsalted butter, cut into small pieces

Bake until bubbly and browned on top, 7 to 10 minutes (opposite).

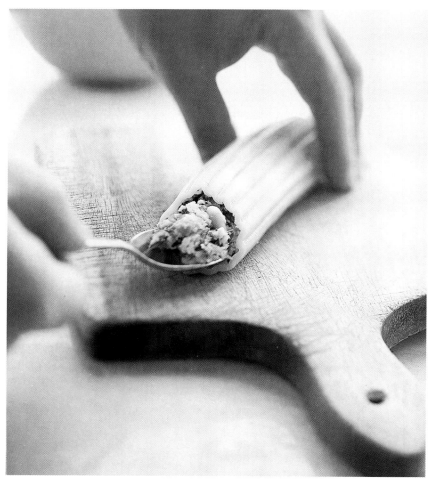

Baked Manicotti

6 to 8 servings

Have ready:
Italian Tomato Sauce, 36
Simple Cheese Filling, 66

Bring to a rolling boil in a large pot:

8 litres (13 pints) water
2 tbsp salt

Add and cook until barely tender:

500g (1lb) manicotti or canelloni

Preheat the oven to 180°C (350°F) Gas 4. Lightly oil a 3 litre (5 pint) shallow baking dish. Using a small spoon, fill the pasta tubes with the cheese filling. Arrange the rolls side by side in the baking dish. At this point, the dish can be covered and refrigerated for up to 24 hours. Just before baking, spoon the tomato sauce over the manicotti and sprinkle with:

60g (2oz) grated mozzarella cheese
3 tbsp grated Parmesan or Asiago cheese

Cover with foil and bake until heated through, about 40 minutes. Let stand for 10 minutes in the turned-off oven with the door open. Serve hot.

Making Crêpes

Crêpes are most easily made in a crêpe pan – a short-sided frying pan about 19cm (7½ in) across. (You can also use a normal frying pan of the same size.) If your pan is non-stick, you may not have to season it – simply follow the manufacturer's instructions. New crêpe pans always need to be seasoned. Rub the surface lightly with corn or sunflower oil, then wipe off any excess. Once seasoned, crêpe pans do not have to be washed; a quick wipe with a paper towel keeps them in good shape.

You will need only 2 to 3 tablespoons of batter for each crêpe. The easiest and neatest way to get this small amount of batter into the pan is to pour it from a jug or from a ladle that holds just the right amount. Heat a crêpe pan over medium to medium-high heat and rub the end of a block of butter on the cooking surface. Lift the pan off the heat and pour in the batter, tilting and rotating the pan as you do so that the batter covers the entire bottom of the pan in a very thin, even layer. Cook the crêpe on one side until it sets and starts to bubble (the underside should be golden brown). Run a blunt, thin knife or long palette knife around the edge of the pan, lift the crêpe up and turn it over. Cook the second side just until it is speckled with golden dots; it will never be as brown as the first side.

Basic Savoury Crêpes

About twelve 19cm (7½ in) crêpes

Combine in a blender or food processor until smooth:
75g (2½ oz) plain flour
125ml (4floz) milk
60ml (2floz) lukewarm water
2 large eggs
30g (1oz) unsalted butter, melted
½ tsp salt

Pour the batter into a jug or other container with a pouring lip. Cover with cling film and let stand for 30 minutes or refrigerate for up to 2 days. (This allows the flour to thoroughly absorb the liquid and gives the gluten in the flour a chance to relax.)

Place a nonstick or seasoned crêpe pan over medium heat. Coat the pan with a little:
Unsalted butter

Stir the batter and pour about 2 tbsp into the pan, lifting the pan off the heat and tilting and rotating it so that the batter forms an even, very thin layer. Cook until the top is set and the underside is golden. Turn the crêpe over, using a palette knife or your fingers (fingers work best here) and cook until the second side is lightly browned. Remove the crêpe to a piece of greaseproof paper. Continue cooking the rest of the crêpes, buttering the pan and stirring the batter before starting each one. Stack the finished crêpes between sheets of greaseproof paper. Use immediately or let cool, wrap airtight, and freeze for up to 1 month.

STORING CRÊPE BATTER AND FINISHED CRÊPES

Crêpe batter can be made up to 2 days ahead and kept in a bowl, covered, in the refrigerator. Give the batter a good stirring before you start cooking. Crêpes can be served as soon as they are made but typically are kept aside to be served all together. Place the first crêpe on a plate and cover with greaseproof paper. Continue layering the crêpes between sheets of paper as they are cooked.

To store, cover the plate with cling film and refrigerate overnight, or wrap the crêpes airtight and freeze for up to 1 month. Crêpes can be thawed, still wrapped, overnight in the refrigerator. Or warm in a microwave for a few seconds – just to make them soft enough to peel from the greaseproof paper without tearing.

Crespelle

6 servings

Have ready:

Eight 18cm (7in) Basic Savoury Crêpes, opposite, or Buckwheat Crêpes, right
Simple Cheese Filling, 66, Meat Filling, 67 or Vegetable Cheese Filling, 66
Italian Tomato Sauce, 36

Preheat the oven to 180°C (350°F) Gas 4. Grease a 2½ litre (4 pint) shallow baking dish. Spread the filling over the crêpes. Roll up and arrange side by side in the dish. Cover with foil and bake for 15 minutes. Pour the tomato sauce over the crêpes and bake, uncovered, until the sauce is bubbling and the crêpes are heated through, about 10 minutes more. Serve hot.

Buckwheat Crêpes

About 16 crêpes

Buckwheat crêpes, also known as galettes de sarrasin, are a little thicker than standard wheat flour crêpes. They are also a lot more assertive, thanks to the strong, nutlike flavour of buckwheat. Rarely used in desserts, buckwheat crêpes can be used in any savoury crêpes recipe. The batter needs to rest for an hour before cooking the crêpes, remember to allow for this in your timing.

Combine in a blender or food processor until smooth:
90g (3oz) buckwheat flour
75g (2½oz) plain flour

250ml (8floz) milk
180ml (6floz) water
3 large eggs
2 tbsp vegetable oil
1 tsp salt

Scrape down the sides of the container with a rubber spatula and process until thoroughly blended, about 15 seconds more.

Pour the crêpe batter into a jug or other container with a pouring lip. Cover with cling film and let stand for 1 hour or refrigerate for up to 1 day. Proceed as for *Basic Savoury Crêpes, opposite.*

ABOUT **WESTERN** NOODLES

*N*oodles have long been popular food all over Europe, and first travelled to America with settlers from Holland and Germany. Later a broad array of other noodle favourites from Russia, Hungary and Ukraine were also adopted. While their origins can often be forgotten, these dishes, with their quirky names, variable shapes, and soft to chewy textures, offer a great deal of pleasure and nourishment.

They also offer an abundance of variety in the ways they may be enjoyed. You could serve Egg Noodles with Garlic and Breadcrumbs, *83, for example, as a first course. For an easy main course, try the recipe in this section for* Baked Macaroni and Cheese, *88. The Jewish noodle puddings known as kugels, 85, are often served with robust main courses such as braised beef or roast chicken.*

Egg Noodles with Sour Cream and Chives, 83

Egg Noodles

500g (1lb)

These are rich and savoury egg noodles.

BY HAND:

In a large bowl, cut together with a pastry blender or your fingers to form fine crumbs:

235g (7½ oz) plain flour

15g (½oz) plus 1 tsp cold unsalted butter

⅛ tsp salt

Make a well in the centre. Lightly beat together and add to the well:

2 large egg yolks

2 large eggs

Using a fork, gradually mix the flour mixture into the eggs, and continue to mix until the dough comes together. Divide the dough into quarters. Start rolling out 1 piece of the dough with a rolling pin, stretching it a little more with each roll. Between each rolling and stretching, continue to sprinkle it with flour if needed to keep it from sticking. Repeat this procedure until the dough is paper thin and translucent. Repeat with the remaining dough. Let it dry on a pasta rack or makeshift dowel for about 20 minutes. Avoid drying the noodles too much. Roll the noodle sheets up and cut to the desired thickness. The noodle dough can also be rolled and cut with a hand-cranked pasta machine; follow the manufacturer's instructions.

IN A FOOD PROCESSOR:

Cut the butter into very small pieces and place in the bowl with the flour and salt. Pulse 2 or 3 times to mix. Add the eggs and pulse again to mix the dough. The dough should form a ball around the blade. Do not overmix. Roll out as directed above.

Buttered Egg Noodles

6 to 8 servings

This easy noodle recipe will keep the kids at the supper table.

Bring to a rolling boil in a large saucepan:

3 litres (5 pints) water

1 tbsp salt

Add and cook until tender but firm:

500g (1lb) *Egg Noodles, left,* **or 500g (1lb) dried**

Fresh noodles will take as long as 5 minutes, depending upon how thick they are. If using dried noodles, follow the package directions. Drain the noodles and return to the pot. Add:

125g (4oz) unsalted butter, melted

Salt and ground black pepper to taste

Toss to coat and serve in warmed bowls or as a side dish.

Egg Noodles with Sour Cream and Chives

6 to 8 servings

Combine in a medium saucepan:

125g (4oz) unsalted butter, melted
250g (8oz) sour cream or yoghurt
45g (1½oz) chopped onion
2 tbsp finely snipped fresh chives
2 tbsp chopped fresh parsley
1 clove garlic, finely chopped

Cook gently for about 5 minutes.

Toss with:

500g (1lb) *Egg Noodles, opposite,*
or 500g (1lb) dried egg noodles,
cooked until tender but firm

Serve immediately.

Egg Noodles with Garlic and Breadcrumbs

6 to 8 servings

Melt in a medium frying pan until the foam subsides:

60-125g (2-4oz) unsalted butter

Add:

90g (3oz) dry breadcrumbs
1-2 cloves garlic, finely chopped

Cook, stirring, until the breadcrumbs begin to brown. Stir in:

1 tbsp chopped fresh parsley

Toss with:

500g (1lb) *Egg Noodles, opposite,*
or 500g (1lb) dried egg noodles,
cooked until tender but firm

Serve immediately.

Egg Noodles with Curd Cheese

6 to 8 servings

If you can't find curd cheese, use cottage cheese.

Toss together in the noodle cooking pot:

500g (1lb) *Egg Noodles, opposite,* or
500g (1lb) dried egg noodles,
cooked until tender but firm
125g (4oz) unsalted butter, melted
500g (1lb) curd or cottage cheese
Salt and ground black pepper
to taste

Heat through over low heat. Serve garnished with:

Crumbled bacon (optional)
Chopped fresh parsley or snipped
fresh dill

Poppy-Seed Noodles

6 to 8 servings

Serve these noodles (above) as an accompaniment to braised or stewed meats or as a simple main dish on their own. With sugar added, they could even be enjoyed for dessert.

Toss together:

500g (1lb) *Egg Noodles, opposite,* or
500g (1lb) dried egg noodles,
cooked until tender but firm
125g (4oz) unsalted butter, melted
2 tbsp poppy seeds, or to taste
1 tsp sugar (optional)

Serve immediately.

Mushroom Walnut Noodle Pudding (Kugel)

10 to 12 servings

This kugel (opposite) can be served as a side dish with meat or poultry or as a main dish for brunch or lunch.

Preheat the oven to 180°C (350°F) Gas 4. Grease a 33 x 23cm (13 x 9in) baking pan with vegetable lard. Bring to a rolling boil in a large pot:

875ml (28floz) chicken broth
1 litre (32floz) water

Add and cook just until tender, 6 to 7 minutes:

375g (12oz) Egg Noodles, 82, or
  375g (12oz) dried egg noodles

Drain. Meanwhile, heat in a large frying pan over medium-high heat:

125ml (4floz) vegetable oil

Add:

2 medium onions, thinly sliced

Cook, stirring, until golden brown, about 10 minutes. Remove with a slotted spoon. Mix 2 tablespoons of the onion cooking oil with the drained noodles to keep them from sticking. Heat the baking pan in the oven for 15 minutes. Add to the remaining oil in the pan:

1 large portobello mushroom cap, wiped clean, sliced, and cut into 2.5cm (1in) pieces
250g (8oz) button mushrooms, wiped clean and sliced
Salt and ground black pepper to taste

Cook, stirring, over medium-high heat until browned, about 10 minutes. Beat well but not until frothy:

5 large eggs, at room temperature

Add the eggs to the noodles and stir together well. Stir in the onions, mushrooms and oil from the frying pan along with:

90g (3oz) roughly chopped walnuts

Pour the noodle mixture into the hot baking pan. Bake until the noodles are lightly browned, about 45 minutes. Serve hot or warm.

PORTOBELLO MUSHROOMS

Portobellos are cultivated, full-blown button mushrooms. They are generous in size (up to 15cm/6in wide), meaty and robustly flavoured (although they have no wild taste). Their open gills and large, flat caps make them naturals for grilling and barbecuing.

Sweet Noodle Pudding (Lukshenkugel)

12 to 14 servings

Some variety of noodle pudding is served at most traditional Jewish holiday meals, and there are countless recipes for them. The custom is to serve a sweet pudding as a second main course on the Sabbath to symbolize prosperity and abundance. Fat-free dairy products can be substituted. This dish is wonderful hot, warm, or cold.

Preheat the oven to 165°C (325°F) Gas 3. Butter a 33 x 23cm (13 x 9in) baking pan. Bring to a rolling boil in a large pot:

6 litres (10 pints) water
2 tbsp salt

Add and cook until tender but firm:

500g (1lb) Egg Noodles, 82, or
  500g (1lb) dried egg noodles

Drain. Stir together in a large bowl:

500ml (16floz) sour cream
500g (1lb) cottage cheese
500g (1lb) cream cheese
3 large eggs
125g (4oz) sugar
2 tsp vanilla
1 tsp ground cinnamon
½ tsp salt

Add the noodles and stir together well. Pour into the baking pan. Bake for 1½ hours. Meanwhile, stir together in a small bowl with a fork or your fingers:

100g (3½ oz) dark brown sugar
60g (2oz) chopped walnuts
2 tbsp plain flour
2 tsp ground cinnamon
30g (1oz) butter, softened

Sprinkle over the top of the casserole and bake for 30 minutes more.

Tuna Noodle Casserole

4 to 6 servings

This casserole is made with a cheese sauce studded with vegetables. It takes only a few minutes more to make than the condensed-soup kind, and the results are much more rewarding.
Position a rack in the centre of the oven. Preheat the oven to 190°C (375°F) Gas 5. Butter a 1.5-2 litre (2½-3 pint) shallow baking dish. To make the roux (opposite) melt in a medium saucepan over medium heat until fragrant and bubbly:

60g (2oz) unsalted butter
Add:
90g (3oz) thinly sliced mushrooms
60g (2oz) finely diced red or green peppers
60g (2oz) chopped onion

Cook, stirring occasionally, until the vegetables are just tender, about 5 minutes. Stir in:

4 tbsp plain flour
Cook for 1 minute. Remove from the heat and whisk in:

625ml (1 pint) milk
Return the saucepan to the heat and cook, whisking, until the sauce comes to a boil and is thickened, about 10 minutes. Remove from the heat, add, and whisk until melted:

60-90g (2-3oz) grated Cheddar cheese
Drain thoroughly:

Two 185g (6oz) tins tuna
Turn the tuna into a large bowl and break into flakes with a fork. Do not

mince. Stir in the hot cheese sauce, then add:

375g (12oz) cooked egg noodles
4 tbsp chopped fresh parsley
Salt and ground black pepper to taste
Stir together well. Pour the mixture into the baking dish. Mix together and sprinkle over the top:

45g (1½oz) dry breadcrumbs or crushed corn flakes
30g (1oz) unsalted butter, melted
Bake until bubbly and browned on top, 25 to 35 minutes.

MAKING A ROUX

A roux is a mixture of fat and flour, cooked together, usually in equal amounts. Although exact amounts of fat and flour are called for in recipes, it is solely the amount of flour that determines the thickness of the sauce. Fat lubricates and smooths the flour so it does not form lumps when combined with stock or other liquid. The preferred fat is butter, but it could also be chicken or other poultry fat, rendered meat drippings, oil or margarine.

A roux is started by melting butter or other fat, adding flour and cooking the two together over low heat, whisking or stirring constantly to prevent scorching. During this process, which takes only a few minutes, the starch in the flour expands as it blends with the fat; if a roux cooks too quickly, the resulting mixture will be grainy. (If the fat floats to the top, the roux has separated; this happens rarely, but if it does, there is nothing to do but to throw out the roux and start again.)

There are three types of roux – white, blonde, and brown, each with a different cooking time. White roux, used to make traditional white sauce, should be cooked just until the butter and flour are evenly incorporated and smooth and should be removed from the heat before the roux begins to darken at all, 3 to 5 minutes (**1**). Blonde roux, used in velouté-based sauces and cream soups, cooks for a little longer, until it begins to give off a faint nutty aroma and turns an ivory colour, 6 to 7 minutes (**2**). Brown roux, basic to Cajun and Creole cooking, cooks the longest – 8 to 15 minutes and sometimes longer – until it is a dark brown and has a strong nutty fragrance (**3**). (The longer you cook a roux, the less it will thicken. The heat eventually breaks down the starch in the flour.)

Whether making white, blonde or brown roux, let it cool slightly before slowly whisking in the stock or other liquid. If you have made the roux in advance, it is important to first warm either it or the liquid to be added to it. The legendary rule is to add hot liquid to cold roux or cold liquid to hot roux. The important thing to remember is to avoid trying to combine cold roux and cold liquid, which would become lumpy, or hot roux and hot liquid, which would spatter. Once the roux and liquid are combined, stir constantly until the sauce is thickened and comes to a simmer. Once it has thickened, stir and skim often during the slow, gentle cooking needed to reduce the sauce to the desired consistency. Any trace of a floury taste will disappear after 10 minutes of slow simmering. If lumps do appear, strain the sauce through a fine-mesh sieve before proceeding.

The pan in which you make a roux should be chosen carefully. In order to prevent scorching, use a saucepan or frying pan with a heavy bottom. Some cooks prefer enamel-covered cast iron, and others cast iron au naturel.

Baked Macaroni and Cheese

4 to 6 main-course servings; 8 to 10 side-dish servings

An especially good rendition of a timeless classic (opposite). The sauce can be made ahead and blended with just-cooked noodles before baking, or the entire casserole can be assembled a day ahead of time. As the reduced-fat variation, right, proves, it is possible to enjoy this classic comfort food even if you are trying to restrict calories and fat.

Preheat the oven to 180°C (350°F) Gas 4. Grease a 1.5 litre (2½ pint) deep baking dish. Bring to a rolling boil in a medium saucepan:

1.5 litres (2½ pints) water
1½ tsp salt
Add and cook just until tender:
250g (8oz) macaroni
Drain and remove to a large bowl. Have ready:
220g (7oz) grated mature Cheddar cheese
Melt in a large saucepan over medium-low heat:

30g (1oz) butter
Whisk in and cook, whisking, for 3 minutes:
2 tbsp plain flour
Gradually whisk in:
500ml (16floz) milk
Stir in:
½ medium onion, chopped
1 bay leaf
¼ tsp sweet paprika
Simmer gently, stirring often, for 15 minutes. Remove from the heat and stir in two-thirds of the cheese. Season with:
Salt and ground black pepper to taste
Stir in the macaroni. Pour half of the mixture into the baking dish and sprinkle with half of the remaining cheese. Top with the remaining macaroni and then the remaining cheese. Melt in a small frying pan over medium heat:

15g (½ oz) butter
Add and toss to coat:
45g (1½oz) fresh breadcrumbs
Sprinkle over the top of the macaroni. Bake until the breadcrumbs are lightly browned, about 30 minutes. Let stand for 5 minutes before serving.

BAKED MACARONI AND CHEESE (REDUCED-FAT)

Prepare Baked Macaroni and Cheese, left, using skimmed milk instead of whole milk and substituting 250g (8oz) reduced fat Cheddar cheese for the mature Cheddar. Cut the cheese into 2.5cm (1in) cubes and add them to the sauce all at once before seasoning with salt and ground black pepper to taste.

Stovetop Macaroni and Cheese

4 to 6 main-course servings; 8 to 10 side-dish servings

This noodle dish is very creamy and very cheesy. The size of the pot is essential in this recipe – it must be big for the sauce to thicken correctly. If you do not have a 7 litre (12 pint) pot, you can cook the macaroni in any pot; then prepare the cheese sauce on its own in a 30cm (12in) frying pan and, once it has thickened to the desired consistency, add the cooked pasta and stir to coat it well before serving.

Bring to a rolling boil in a large pot:
3 litres (5 pints) water
1 tbsp salt
Add and cook just until tender:

250g (8oz) macaroni
Drain and return to the pot. Add:
60g (2oz) unsalted butter, cut into small pieces
Stir until well blended. Add and stir together until smooth:
375ml (12floz) evaporated milk
375g (12oz) extra mature Cheddar cheese, grated
2 large eggs, lightly beaten
1 tsp dried mustard powder dissolved in 1 tsp water
¾ tsp salt
½ tsp cayenne pepper, or to taste

Set the pot over very low heat and, stirring constantly, bring the mixture to the first bubble of a simmer, 5 to 10 minutes. It should thicken noticeably. This may take several minutes. Increase the heat slightly if the sauce is still soupy after 5 minutes, but watch it very carefully. Do not overheat (above 76°C/ 170°F), or the sauce will curdle. Serve immediately. If you are not ready to serve, remove the pot from the heat, cover the surface with cling film, cover the pot and let stand at room temperature.

ABOUT **ORIENTAL** NOODLES

In over two thousand years of noodle making, cooks in China, Japan, Thailand, Vietnam and other Oriental countries have come up with a wondrous variety of recipes. Today, many of these — pan-fried noodles, ramen noodle soup, pad thai and lo mein — are becoming favourites in our busy lives here in the Western world.

Oriental noodles are best understood by the type of flour or starch with which they are made. When looking for substitutes, choose noodles in the same starch family. Today, the most common Oriental noodles are made with wheat or rice; some are also made from mung bean starch and buckwheat. In general, ignore the recipe directions on the package and follow the advice given here, along with your own good sense. Orientals prefer noodles long and uncut, because they symbolize longevity, especially when served at birthday celebrations. Eating noodles in the East can be a noisy affair: it is not impolite to slurp them up.

Singapore Noodles, 100

Oriental Noodles

CHINESE WHEAT FLOUR NOODLES

Fresh wheat noodles come in a variety of shapes and thicknesses, including a spaghetti shape and a thick oval-shaped strand, known as Shanghai style. More unusual, but equally delicious, is the flat, wide wheat chow fun. Dried Chinese wheat noodles are packaged in straight 30cm (12in) lengths or, in the case of thinner noodles, in nests. Generally, Chinese wheat flour noodles are used in soups and sometimes in stir-fried dishes. Cook by dropping the noodles into a large pot of boiling water (without salt or oil) until softened, about 4 minutes (longer for dried). The Chinese like to cook their noodles until they are very tender. Before stir-frying or adding to soup, rinse the cooked noodles under cold water and toss with a little oil to prevent them from clumping.

CHINESE EGG NOODLES

Fresh and dried egg noodles are made with wheat flour and eggs. The best are pale yellow in colour and have a dry, fresh look. Chinese egg noodles are popularly sold as mein. Regular mein, about 3mm (⅛ in) thick, resembles spaghetti and is used for stir-frying (as in lo mein), for pan-frying, or in cold noodle dishes. Egg noodles are also available thin or extra thin for soups. A flat, fettuccine-like noodle is best stir-fried or cooked and topped with a sauce. Similar egg noodles are called ramen in Japan and ba mee in Thailand. Cook egg noodles according to the directions for Chinese Wheat Flour Noodles, left.

DRIED RICE FLOUR NOODLES

Noodles made with rice flour and water are among the most popular of all Oriental noodles. They are sold in 500g (1lb) packets in Chinese, Thai and Vietnamese shops in two basic styles – rice sticks and rice vermicelli.

RICE STICK NOODLES

These thin, flat, translucent noodles should be soaked for 30 minutes in cold water, then boiled for 4 to 7 minutes before being added to any dish. They are most commonly used in pad thai and other stir-fried dishes and soups. Rice sticks are known as banh pho in Vietnam and jantabon in Thailand.

RICE VERMICELLI

These delicate, extra-thin noodles are used in soups, salads and stir-fried dishes. Soak them in cold water for 30 minutes, rinse and then boil for 2 minutes before using. Rice vermicelli can also be deep-fried to make a light, crisp nest on which to serve other foods. If they are to be deep-fried, do not soak or rinse; simply drop the dry noodles into very hot oil, where they will puff and crisp up nicely. Rice vermicelli are bun in Vietnam and san mee in Thailand.

FRESH RICE NOODLES

Most often sold in 500g (1lb) sheets, called sha he fen by the Chinese, these can be cut to any width and used in any dish calling for rice noodles. These versatile noodles will keep refrigerated for up to 2 weeks. After rinsing briefly in warm water, the fresh rice noodles can be stir-fried or added directly to soups without cooking them first.

MUNG BEAN NOODLES

Called cellophane noodles or bean threads, these translucent dried noodles are made from the starch of the mung bean and sold in small bundles. Popular in soups and occasionally stir-fried, these threadlike noodles have a more slippery texture than either rice or wheat noodles. Cellophane noodles also puff up into a crisp nest when deep-fried. These should be soaked in hot water to soften for 15 to 30 minutes before using (unless headed to the deep fryer) and then can be added directly to a soup or stir-fry.

JAPANESE UDON NOODLES

Thick, plump, white noodles made of wheat flour, salt and water, udon come both flat and round, dried and fresh, and are first cousins to the Shanghai-style wheat flour noodle. Typically served in broth and sprinkled with chopped spring onions and a fiery spice mixture called shichimi, these hearty noodles also work well in gutsy stews and casseroles.

Clockwise from top left (opposite): mung bean noodles, udon, dried rice noodles, rice stick noodles, Chinese egg noodles, rice vermicelli, Chinese wheat flour noodles, fresh rice noodles, ramen (centre)

Oriental Ingredients

BAMBOO SHOOTS

Rinse tinned bamboo shoots well before using; if you cannot use the whole tin, transfer the remaining shoots to a covered container of fresh water and try to change the water daily. Fresh bamboo shoots, the new growth of bamboo stalks, are a marvelous addition to stir-fries. These are usually available only in winter and are hard to find even then. Unpeeled fresh shoots will keep for a week in the refrigerator. To use, peel away the outer leaves, cut off and discard the base and cook the edible inner core, whole or sliced, in boiling water for at least 5 minutes to remove a toxin, hydrocyanic acid. If the shoot still tastes bitter, boil it again. Drain, rinse and refrigerate in water as for tinned. Bamboo shoots are so bland that their value is texture rather than flavour. They blend especially well with other Oriental vegetables, ancient companions. In a mix, allow about 60g (2oz) per serving.

BOK CHOY, OR PAK CHOI

It is confusing when bok choy is called pak choi – and the reverse. The names not only sound similar, but, in fact, they refer to the same vegetable, a mild-flavoured Chinese cabbage (above). By and large these plants have pale green to white stalks and rich green leaves. Select medium-sized bunches with the brightest colours and firmest stalks. Very small bunches will be labelled baby bok choy. In spring and summer, you may find flowering bok choy, bunches with small broccoli-like florets. Store in perforated plastic vegetable bags in the refrigerator vegetable drawer.

CHINESE COOKING WINE

Shaoxing (Shaoshing) wine, China's most famous rice wine, from Shaoshing, in the eastern province of Zhejiang, has been made, it is said, for more than 2,000 years. Blended glutinous rice, rice millet, a special yeast and local mineral and spring waters give this amber-coloured beverage its unique flavour. More like sherry in colour, bouquet, and alcohol content (18 percent) than like sake or a grape wine, it is aged at least ten years in earthenware and in underground cellars. The finest varieties are aged a century or more. Like sake, Shaoshing is usually drunk warm and is rarely left out of a dish; it is vital to Chinese cooking from stir-fries to stews to such famous specialities as "drunken" chicken. A top-quality dry sherry is a good substitute.

OYSTER SAUCE

Originally made from oysters, water and salt only, oyster sauce now contains added cornflour and caramel colour, to improve its appearance. When buying oyster sauce, avoid the cheaper varieties, which contain fewer oysters and more cornflour. Store it in the refrigerator.

PEANUT OIL

Peanut oil varies greatly in quality. When it has not been cold pressed (and most peanut oil has not been), there is little or no peanut flavour. In Asian supermarkets, you can find cold-pressed oils with a true peanut taste.

SESAME OIL

In China, sesame oil is considered too expensive to cook with, but it is highly prized as a seasoning sprinkled over dishes just at the end of cooking. The best sesame oil is pressed from seeds that have first been toasted. In Japan, tempura oil may contain up to one-half sesame oil and is suitable for deep-frying; sesame oil on its own burns too quickly to stand up to this kind of heat.

SOY SAUCE

Soy sauce is a naturally fermented product made in several steps and aged up to two years. Typically, roasted soybean meal and a lightly ground grain are mixed with an *Aspergillis* mould starter. Brine is then added to the fermented meal, along with a *Lactobacillus* starter and yeast. The mash is then aged slowly. When the producer decides it is ready, the soy sauce is then strained and bottled.

Chinese Soy Sauce: The Chinese use light and dark soy sauces. The latter is aged longer and towards the end of the processing is mixed with bead molasses, which gives it a dark caramel hue.

Japanese Soy Sauce: The technique of aging and fermenting is the same for Japanese and Chinese soy sauces, but as a rule Japanese soy sauce (*shoyu*) contains more wheat and is thus a little sweeter and less salty.

Clockwise from top left: dark soy sauce, light soy sauce, oyster sauce, Chinese cooking wine, sesame oil, peanut oil

Chicken Lo Mein

4 servings

Lo mein simply means sautéed noodles. Fresh Chinese egg noodles are traditional, but any spaghetti-shaped noodle works well. You could also use dried linguine. Almost any combination of meat and vegetables can be added.

BEFORE COOKING:

Stir together in a medium bowl:

1 tsp cornflour

½ tsp salt

1 tsp toasted sesame oil

Cut across the grain to make very thin slices (more easily done if the chicken is partially frozen):

1 boneless, skinless chicken breast (about 185g/6oz)

Toss in the cornflour mixture and let marinate for 10 to 20 minutes. Place on a plate:

125g (4oz) bok choy, cut crosswise into 7.5cm (3in) pieces

45g (1½oz) bamboo shoots, sliced

3 spring onions, cut into 5cm (2in) pieces

30g (1oz) sliced mushrooms

1 tsp finely chopped garlic

Stir together in a small bowl:

60ml (2floz) *Chicken Stock*, 17

2 tbsp oyster sauce

1 tbsp light or dark soy sauce

1½ tsp sugar

Have ready:

4 tbsp bean sprouts

TO COOK:

Bring to a rolling boil in a large pot:

4 litres (6½ pints) water

Add and cook until softened:

185g (6oz) fresh Chinese egg noodles or dried spaghetti

Drain and rinse under cold water until cool. Drain again and toss thoroughly with:

1 tsp toasted sesame oil

Heat a wok or large frying pan over high heat. When hot, pour in:

80ml (3floz) peanut oil

Swirl around the wok until very hot but not smoking. Add the chicken, quickly stirring and flipping in the oil to separate the slices, and cook lightly. Drain in a sieve or colander. Reheat the wok over high heat. When hot, pour in:

3 tbsp peanut oil

Swirl until very hot but not smoking. Add all the ingredients on the plate with the bok choy. Stir and toss vigorously until the vegetables are well coated with oil, about 45 seconds. Pour the chicken stock mixture down the side of the wok. Stir and cover, allowing the vegetables to steam in the sauce, for 1 minute. Uncover and add the noodles and the chicken. Stir and toss for about 30 seconds. Add the bean sprouts and stir for about 30 seconds. Pour into a serving dish. Sprinkle with:

½ tsp cracked black peppercorns

Serve immediately.

Beef Chow Fun

4 servings

Chow fun *usually implies pan-fried broad rice noodles. This dish is typical Chinese noodle-house fare.*

BEFORE COOKING:

Soak in hot water to cover until softened, about 20 minutes:

250g (8oz) dried rice noodles, 1cm (½ in) wide

Stir together well in a medium bowl:

2 tsp light or dark soy sauce

1 tsp cornflour

Stir in:

1 tsp toasted sesame oil

Cut across the grain to make very thin 5 x 2.5cm (2 x 1in) slices (more easily done if the meat is partially frozen):

250g (8oz) rump steak

Toss in the soy mixture and let marinate for 20 to 30 minutes.

Place on a saucer or small plate:

2 tsp Chinese salted black beans, lightly mashed

2 tsp finely chopped garlic

4 tsp finely chopped peeled fresh ginger

Place on a separate plate:

250g (8oz) green beans, trimmed and cut into 5cm (2in) pieces

Place on another plate:

3 fresh red chillies, or ½ red pepper for less heat, cut into thin strips

60g (2oz) spring onions, cut into 5cm (2in) pieces

Stir together in a small bowl:

125ml (4floz) Chicken Stock, 17

60ml (2floz) oyster sauce

2 tbsp Chinese cooking wine or dry white wine

2 tbsp light or dark soy sauce

2 tsp sugar

Stir together well in a cup, leaving the stirring spoon in for later:

2 tsp cornflour

2 tbsp cool water

Have ready:

1 tsp toasted sesame oil

TO COOK:

Heat a wok or large frying pan over high heat. When hot, pour in:

125ml (4floz) peanut oil

Swirl around the wok until very hot but not smoking. Add the beef, quickly stirring and flipping in the oil to separate the slices, and cook lightly. Drain in a sieve or colander. Drain the noodles well. Reheat the wok or frying pan over high heat.

When hot, pour in:

60ml (2floz) peanut oil

Swirl until hot. Add the noodles. From time to time, stir and toss until some surfaces brown slightly. Remove to a plate. Discard the oil. Reheat the wok over high heat. When hot, pour in:

60ml (2floz) peanut oil

Swirl until very hot but not smoking. Scrape in the black beans, garlic and ginger. Stir briefly until the garlic browns very slightly. Add the green beans and toss for 1 minute. Add the chillies and spring onions and stir well for 1 minute more.

Stir the chicken stock mixture and add. Stir and toss until completely hot. Return the beef and noodles to the wok. Stir and toss quickly to mix completely.

Stir the cornflour mixture. Pour it slowly into the sauce while stirring. Stir until the mixture is thickened and the noodles are glazed and shiny. Add the sesame oil and give a final stir.

Pour into a serving dish. Top with:

Fresh coriander leaves

Serve immediately.

FERMENTED BLACK BEANS

These soybeans, partially decomposed by means of a special mould, then dried and sometimes salted, predate soy sauce; in fact, scholars say they may have been the very first soy food. Fermented black beans have a pleasing winy flavour and when used properly are a wonderful complement to seafood and meats. Rinsing fermented black beans is unnecessary. When buying the salted kind, simply take their saltiness into account when adding other seasonings. Depending on the dish, fermented black beans should be chopped lightly or crushed a little with the side of a cleaver to release their flavour, then tossed with a tablespoon or two of Shaoshing wine or dry sherry, and chopped garlic and ginger if the dish calls for them, and set aside until ready to use. Fermented black beans, often flavoured with bits of ginger and sometimes orange peel, are usually sold in 250g (8oz) packets. Choose those that feel soft when you touch the bag. After the packet is opened, they should be transferred to a covered jar and stored at room temperature away from light and heat. They will keep indefinitely.

Singapore Noodles

4 servings

This popular Chinese version of a Malaysian dish uses curry powder and thin rice noodles. Traditionally it is made with Chinese barbecued pork, cha siu; here we use loin of pork.

BEFORE COOKING:

Soak in hot water to cover until softened, about 10 minutes:

250g (8oz) thin rice vermicelli

Drain. Cut into thin slices and then into thin strips (more easily done if the meat is partially frozen):

125g (4oz) loin of pork

Combine in a small bowl with:

2 tsp light or dark soy sauce

Toss and let stand.

Place on one side of a plate:

30g (1oz) thinly sliced onion

1 tsp thin strips fresh red chilli

Warm in a small frying pan over low heat:

2 tbsp curry powder

Stir in:

60ml (2floz) unsweetened coconut milk

1 tsp salt

½ tsp sugar

Cook, stirring, for 30 to 45 seconds. Scrape the mixture into a second small bowl.

Stir together in a third small bowl:

60ml (2floz) *Chicken Stock, 17*

1 tbsp oyster sauce

1 tsp salt

Place on the other side of the plate:

30g (1oz) roasted peanuts, chopped

1 tsp crushed chilli flakes

2 tbsp dried prawns, very finely chopped (optional)

Stir together well in a fourth small bowl:

155g (5oz) bean sprouts

2 tbsp chopped fresh basil

Juice of ½ lemon

TO COOK:

Heat a wok or large frying pan over high heat. When hot, pour in:

60ml (2floz) peanut oil

Swirl around the wok until very hot but not smoking. Add the pork, quickly stirring and flipping to separate the strips. Cook until they are no longer pink but not browned. Remove with a slotted spoon. To the wok add:

1 tbsp peanut oil

Swirl until very hot. Add the onions and chilli peppers. Cook and stir until the onions are softened, about 5 minutes. Remove with a slotted spoon, leaving as much oil as possible in the wok. Set aside atop the pork strips.

Add the curry mixture to the wok. Stir and cook very briefly. Quickly add the chicken stock mixture and heat through, stirring constantly. Add the noodles, seared pork strips and onion mixture to the wok, stirring constantly until heated through. Add the peanuts, chilli flakes and dried prawns if using, and stir thoroughly.

Add the bean sprout mixture and stir for about 30 seconds, until all the ingredients are thoroughly mixed. Pour into a serving dish. Serve immediately.

CURRY POWDER

Packaged curry powder was most likely a British invention. Hoping to import the flavours enjoyed in India, the British took home with them one of the southern Indian spice mixtures, adding this blend to Western-style flour-bound stews that were then dubbed curries. Indian cooks do not use a single spice mixture. Rather, each dish is flavoured individually with a combination of spices, called a *masala*. *Madras Curry Powder, right,* is a variation on one such blend.

Madras Curry Powder

About 185g (6oz)

You may substitute dried leaves for fresh, but their flavour is much less pungent.

Toast in a heated frying pan over medium heat until a shade darker and fragrant, about 4 minutes:

6 tbsp whole coriander seeds

4 tbsp whole cumin seeds

3 tbsp *chana dal* or yellow split peas

1 tbsp black peppercorns

1 tbsp black mustard seeds

5 dried red chilli peppers

10 fresh or dried curry leaves

Combine the toasted spices with:

2 tbsp fenugreek seeds

Grind to a powder in batches in a spice mill or electric coffee grinder. Mix well with:

3 tbsp turmeric

Store in an airtight container in a cool place.

HOW TO MAKE COCONUT MILK

Under the shell of a coconut lies the skin. The white creamy meat beneath surrounds a pool of milky, faintly sweet liquid, refreshing to drink. Many call this liquid coconut milk. Do not confuse it, however, with the coconut milk called for in recipes, which is an infusion. This infusion can be purchased in tins or in dehydrated blocks or can be made from scratch. Quality varies among shop-bought brands. Try a few to find the brand with the most body and the freshest flavour. To make coconut milk, look for chunks of freshly cracked coconut, with the inner brown skin still attached.

1 Peel away the brown skin attached to the chunks of fresh coconut with a vegetable peeler or a paring knife.

2 Grate the chunks of fresh coconut on the large rasps of a box grater.

3 Pour 250ml (8floz) boiling water or milk over 100g (3½ oz) fresh coconut shreds.

4 Stir well, cover and let steep for 30 minutes. In steeping, the coconut will have infused the liquid with flavour and lent body to it.

5 Process the grated coconut and the soaking liquid, no more than 750ml (24floz) at a time, in a blender or food processor for 1 minute.

6 Pour all the shreds and milk into a damp clean tea towel and press the liquid into a bowl, squeezing until the shreds are dry. Cover the coconut milk, refrigerate and use within 3 days. Once refrigerated, a layer of fat will rise to the top. This is known as coconut cream. It can be skimmed off and refrigerated.

Spicy Peanut Sesame Noodles

4 to 6 servings

This traditional Chinese dish is served at room temperature as an appetizer, a lunch or a light supper. It is a delight of taste and texture, with soft noodles, creamy sauce, spicy chilli peppers, and the crunch of raw cucumbers.

BEFORE COOKING:

Thoroughly blend in a food processor:

315g (10oz) natural unsalted smooth peanut butter
125ml (4floz) rice or white vinegar
60ml (2floz) light soy sauce
2 tsp dark soy sauce
2 tbsp small pieces garlic
2 to 6 serrano or other fresh chilli peppers, cut into pieces

3 tbsp sugar
2 tsp salt

Remove the peanut butter mixture to a medium bowl. Stir in:

125ml (4floz) toasted sesame oil
2 tbsp chilli oil

Gradually stir in until smooth:

250ml (8floz) freshly brewed black tea

The sauce can be covered and refrigerated for 1 to 2 days. Allow to return to room temperature before using.

TO COOK:

Bring to a rolling boil in a large pot:

4-4.5 litres (6½-7 pints) water

Add:

500g (1lb) fresh Chinese egg noodles or dried spaghetti

Cook until softened. Drain and rinse under cold water until cool. Drain and toss thoroughly with:

2 tsp toasted sesame oil

TO SERVE:

Place the noodles in a serving dish, top with all the sauce and stir together slightly. Or serve on individual dinner plates and top with 3 to 4 generous tablespoons of sauce per serving. Garnish with:

Peeled, seeded cucumber, cut into thin strips
Fresh coriander leaves

SPICY PEANUT SESAME NOODLES WITH CHICKEN

Prepare Spicy Peanut Sesame Noodles, above. Poach 2 boneless skinless chicken breasts in boiling water for 5 to 7 minutes. Let cool, shred and stir into the final stage of the sauce.

SERRANO CHILLIES

These tapering, bullet-shaped chillies are prized among cooks for their consistent heat level and pure, fresh chilli taste. Serranos are such a staple in Mexican cooking that they are often called simply *chiles verdes*, or green chillies. Use them fresh, pickled or roasted anywhere their spicy, green, hot pepper qualities are wanted. Widely available in supermarkets today, serranos are mostly sold green, but ripened greenish yellow to red ones can occasionally be found. They measure 4-5cm (1½ -2in) long and 1cm (½ in) wide at the stem end.

RICE VINEGAR

Much of the white rice vinegar produced by Chinese or Japanese manufacturers these days is made from rice wine lees and alcohol. It is pleasant but with less flavour than standard white vinegars, comparable instead to cider vinegar, less the fruitiness and sweetness. Unless a recipe tells you to do otherwise, use the unseasoned variety of rice vinegar.

BREWING TEA

All you need to brew tea well is the best tea you can find and hot water – and the water is almost as important as the tea. If the water that goes into your tea does not taste good, neither will the finished product. Do not use distilled water, because the minerals, essential for flavour, have been removed. Filtered water is ideal.

Your teapot should have a wide mouth, for getting tea in and out of the pot, and a handle that stays cool, left. Orientals tend to prefer clay or iron pots; "brown betty" pots work well, too. Avoid aluminium or any uncoated metal teapots, which will interact with the tea and produce off flavours. Always preheat the teapot, with either boiling water or very hot tap water. Water for brewing most teas must be boiling hot.

The traditional measure for tea is 1 tsp tea per cup and one for the pot, but the amount of tea should vary according to your own taste and the kind of tea you are using. As a starting point, use the above measure for black tea, half again as much for oolong tea and twice as much for green tea. Length of brewing time also varies. Most tea, including tea bags, should steep for at least 3 minutes and no more than 5.

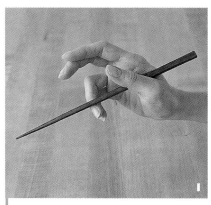

RULES FOR USING CHOPSTICKS

● Unless you are serving a group of specialists, chopsticks should be set in addition to, not instead of, other tableware. If chopsticks are set, they should be placed to the right of the outermost spoon in the table setting. Do not set cheap paper-wrapped wooden chopsticks at a sit-down dinner, though these would be acceptable for a casual lunch. Unwrapped chopsticks are placed side by side, usually with their tips slightly elevated on a small rest (similar to a knife rest, *porte-couteau*).

● To eat with chopsticks, hold them by the upper portion (always thicker than the tip), placing the lower stick in the crease of the thumb, with the lower end of the chopstick braced firmly against the soft inner surface of the last joint of the ring finger (**1**).

● Then position the upper stick much as you would hold a pencil, with the point of the stick approximately even with the lower stick when pressed together at the point (**2**).

● When pressed together, the points of the two chopsticks should be approximately even, and you should be able to grasp the food firmly (**3**).

Shanghai Noodles with Aubergine and Fresh Seasonal Vegetables

4 servings

Traditionally this dish calls for thick hand-cut oval noodles called Shanghai style. They are available fresh in Chinese supermarkets, but good-quality fettuccine, spaghetti or linguine make fine substitutes.

BEFORE COOKING:

Combine in a small bowl:

4 dried mushrooms, preferably Chinese black

500ml (16floz) warm water

Let stand until the mushrooms are softened, 30 to 45 minutes. Drain and squeeze the mushrooms dry with paper towels. Snip off and discard the woody stems. Slice into thin strips.

Peel and cut into 7.5cm (3in) long "French-fry" sticks, about 1cm (⅓ in) thick:

1 small aubergine

Heat a wok or large frying pan over high heat. When hot, pour in:

250ml (8floz) peanut oil

Swirl around the wok until very hot but not smoking. Add the aubergine sticks, moving them gently in the oil to separate. When golden brown, drain in a sieve or colander and immediately set on paper towels. Place on a large plate:

125g (4oz) bok choy, washed, dried and halved lengthwise if necessary

12 fresh mange tout

45g (1½oz) sliced bamboo shoots

3 spring onions, cut into 5cm (2in) pieces

Stir together well in a small bowl:

60ml (2floz) *Chicken Stock, 17*

2 tbsp oyster sauce

1 tbsp light or dark soy sauce

1½ tsp sugar

½ tsp salt

Have ready:

75g (2½ oz) bean sprouts

TO COOK:

Bring to a rolling boil in a large pot:

4 litres (6½ pints) water

Add:

220g (7oz) Shanghai-style noodles

Cook just until tender. Drain and rinse under cold water until cool. Drain and toss thoroughly with:

2 tsp toasted sesame oil

Heat a wok or large frying pan over high heat. When hot, pour in:

3 tbsp peanut oil

Swirl around the wok until very hot but not smoking. Add the mushroom strips and stir briefly.

Add all the ingredients on the plate with the bok choy. Stir and toss vigorously until the vegetables are well coated with oil, about 45 seconds. Pour the chicken stock mixture down the side of the wok. Stir and cover, allowing the vegetables to steam in the sauce until slightly wilted.

Uncover and add the noodles. Stir and toss for about 30 seconds. Add the bean sprouts. Stir for about 30 seconds.

Pour into a serving dish. Distribute the aubergine sticks over the top. Sprinkle with:

¼ tsp cracked black peppercorns

Serve immediately.

Spicy Szechuan Noodles

4 servings

A pork and noodle dish in the Szechuan style, with plenty of fresh ginger, garlic and chilli peppers.

BEFORE COOKING:

Place on a saucer or small plate:

2 tbsp finely chopped peeled fresh ginger

1 tbsp finely chopped garlic

1-2 tbsp coarsely chopped fresh chilli peppers

45g (1½ oz) coarsely chopped bamboo shoots

Stir together well in a small bowl:

60ml (2floz) Chicken Stock, 17

1 tbsp light or dark soy sauce

2 tbsp Chinese black bean sauce

2 tsp sugar

Place on another saucer or small plate:

60g (2oz) spring onions, cut into 5cm (2in) pieces

TO COOK:

Heat a wok or large frying pan over high heat. When hot, pour in:

80ml (3floz) peanut oil

Swirl around the wok until very hot but not smoking. Add all the ingredients on the saucer with the ginger. Stir briefly until the garlic browns very slightly.

Add:

500g (1lb) minced pork

Break up, stir well and cook until the pork is well separated and no longer pink but not browned. Add the chicken stock mixture. Stir well and cook for 1 to 2 minutes. Add the spring onions and stir briefly. Remove the wok from the heat. While cooking the pork, bring to a rolling boil in a large pot:

4-4.5 litres (6½ -7 pints) water

Add:

500g (1lb) fresh Chinese egg noodles or dried spaghetti

Cook until softened. Drain and pour into a large bowl. If necessary, briefly reheat the meat sauce. Pour over the noodles. Season with:

½ tsp toasted sesame oil

Stir together well. Serve immediately.

GINGER

Mistakenly called a root, ginger is a tropical rhizome that is thought to be native to Southeast Asia. If it is fresh and firm, it will keep for a week or so sitting on the counter. To keep it longer, it should go into the vegetable crisper in the refrigerator, inside a perforated plastic bag with a paper towel to absorb any moisture. When buying, select the hardest, heaviest rhizomes; those that have been sitting around will be wrinkled and light in weight. Check where the knobs have been broken: the longer the rhizome has grown before harvesting, the more fibrous it becomes, and the more fibers you will see at the break. Mature fresh ginger is hotter and to some extent more flavourful, but the fibres of an old rhizome may hinder the fine cuts required in Chinese cooking.

BEAN SAUCE

Bean sauce is an essential ingredient in dishes of every region of China. (The beans are soybeans.) You can find it labelled as "whole bean sauce", which has a unique texture, or as "ground bean sauce", which tends to be saltier. All types of bean sauce can be stored indefinitely, tightly covered in the refrigerator.

Beijing Noodles with Meat Sauce

4 servings

Some claim this simple, ancient noodle dish was the original spaghetti with meat sauce. In fact, it is delicious made with spaghetti.

BEFORE COOKING:

Stir together well in a small bowl:

125ml (4floz) Chinese black bean sauce

2 tbsp sugar

Place on a saucer or small plate:

60g (2oz) spring onions cut into 5cm (2in) pieces

Have ready:

1 tbsp toasted sesame oil

TO COOK:

Heat a wok or large frying pan over high heat. When hot, pour in:

3 tbsp peanut oil

Swirl around the wok until very hot but not smoking. Add:

500g (1lb) minced pork

Break up, stir well, and cook until the pork is well separated and no longer pink but not browned. Add the bean sauce mixture. Stir well. Add the spring onions and sesame oil. Stir well.

Remove the wok from the heat. While cooking the pork, bring to a rolling boil in a large pot:

4-4.5 litres (6½ -7 pints) water

Add:

500g (1lb) fresh Chinese egg noodles or dried spaghetti

Cook until softened. Drain and pour into a large bowl. If necessary, briefly reheat the meat sauce. Pour over the noodles and stir well.

TO SERVE:

Stir together in each of 4 small bowls:

60ml (2floz) red wine vinegar

1 tsp chilli oil

Place on the table to be sprinkled onto individual portions to taste.

Chilli Oil

About 180ml (6floz)

Exceedingly hot – use sparingly. A few drops are superb in dipping sauces for dumplings, or in dressings for Oriental vegetable dishes.

Coarsely chop in a blender or spice grinder:

60g (2oz) dried chilli peppers, preferably Thai

Transfer to a stainless-steel saucepan and add:

180ml (6floz) peanut oil

Cook over medium heat until the chillies begin to foam. Remove from the heat when some of the smallest flecks on the side of the pan blacken. Cover, and let sit for 4 to 6 hours. Strain through a dampened paper coffee filter into a scrupulously clean jar or bottle. This keeps, covered and refrigerated, for up to 1 month.

FLAVOURED OILS

Light oils infused with the flavours of herbs, spices and fruits are a refreshing alternative to butter and other fats. Flavoured oils are simple to make at home and add depth of flavour as well as moisture and a sensual touch to finished dishes. It is important to remember that flavoured oils are not for cooking but for seasoning, just as you would drizzle olive oil over vegetables, noodles or pastas. The purest and easiest technique is a cold infusion. Allow ½ to 3 tbsp of oil per serving.

Flavoured oils must be refrigerated, and most will hold their quality for at least 1 month. Prepare only as much as you are likely to use during that period. For optimum flavour, bring the amount of oil you will be serving to room temperature. Leftover warmed oil that has been prepared with fresh (that is, not dried) ingredients must be discarded.

Prawns Pad Thai

4 servings

Rapidly becoming very popular in the West, there are many versions of this Thai specialty. This is a good one. Make an effort to use the optional ingredients – they add body and flavour. Use the red chilli peppers sparingly, unless you like their intense heat.

BEFORE COOKING:

Soak in hot water to cover until softened, 20 to 30 minutes:

185g (6oz) dried rice stick noodles

Drain and cover. Stir together well in a medium bowl:

1 tsp cornflour

1 tsp toasted sesame oil

Peel, devein, and halve lengthwise:

250g (8oz) jumbo prawns

Toss in the cornflour mixture and let marinate for 15 to 20 minutes. Place in a small bowl:

3 large eggs, well beaten

Place on a saucer or small plate:

45g (1½ oz) 4cm (1½ in) pieces spring onion (white part only)

2-3 fresh red chilli peppers, chopped

2 tbsp finely chopped garlic

Place on another saucer or small plate:

125g (4oz) firm tofu, cut into 1cm (½ in) cubes (optional)

Stir together in another small bowl:

60ml (2floz) Thai fish sauce (nam pla)

60ml (2floz) fresh lemon juice

3 tbsp sugar

On a plate, place clockwise from the "top" in the following order:

45g (1½ oz) bean sprouts

45g (1½ oz) roasted peanuts, coarsely chopped

4 tbsp fresh basil leaves, cut into thin strips

4 tbsp fresh coriander leaves

2 tsp dried prawns, finely ground (optional)

½ tsp crushed chilli flakes

½ tsp ground black pepper

TO COOK:

Heat a wok or frying pan over high heat. When hot, pour in:

90ml (3floz) peanut oil

Swirl around the wok until very hot but not smoking. Add the prawns and cook, stirring vigorously, until translucent, 30 to 45 seconds. Drain in a sieve or colander. Reheat the wok over high heat. Pour in:

2 tbsp peanut oil

Swirl briefly. Stir the beaten eggs. Slowly pour the eggs into the wok and cook, stirring vigorously, until the eggs have set. Remove to a plate. Reheat the wok over high heat. When hot, pour in:

3 tbsp peanut oil

Swirl until very hot but not smoking. Add the spring onion mixture and stir briefly until the garlic browns very slightly. Add the tofu if using. Stir gently for 1 to 2 minutes. Add the noodles. Stir until well coated. Add the fish sauce mixture. Stir well. Add the prawns. Add the eggs. Stir well. Add the ingredients on the plate in clockwise order, stirring as you go. Pour into a serving dish. Serve immediately.

CORIANDER

Also known as green cilantro or Chinese parsley but commonly called coriander, these leaves have a piercing flavour. Some perceive the flavour of coriander as a blend hinting of flat-leaf parsley, juniper berries, mint and lovage; others find it a mix of orange peel and sage. Keep in mind that coriander leaves do not hold their flavour when dried. At a pinch, you could substitute flat-leaf parsley for its shape or a spicy basil for its flavour.

HOW TO PEEL AND DEVEIN PRAWNS

You should peel prawns yourself for two reasons: prepeeled prawns have lost some of their flavour, and the shells make great stock. If you are grilling, barbecuing, or boiling prawns, consider cooking them in their shells, as it protects the meat from drying out and helps them retain maximum flavour. You should devein prawns, as the "vein" is actually the intestinal tract and can impart a bitter taste.

1 If the head of the prawn is still attached, break it off at the neck.

2 Peel away the rest of the shell, leaving the tail piece intact.

3 To remove the vein, make a shallow cut along the back of a peeled prawn with a paring knife.

4 Pull out the vein with the tip of the knife.

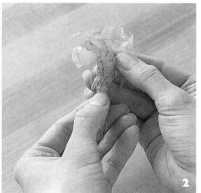

FISH SAUCE

Called nu'o'c ma'm in Vietnam and nam pla in Thailand, fish sauce is made by packing fish, usually anchovies, in crocks or barrels, covering them with brine and allowing them to ferment in the tropical sun over a period of months. The resulting brown liquid is drained off and used. Like olive oil, the first pressing (in this case siphoning), from which flows a clear amber liquid, is most highly prized and is usually reserved for dipping sauces. Subsequent siphonings vary in strength and flavour. Fish sauce is widely available and keeps indefinitely on the shelf.

Pan-Browned Noodle Cake with Prawns and Beef

4 servings

A home-style dish with a noodle "cake" that is golden and crisp on the outside and soft on the inside. It is best made with fresh Chinese egg noodles. Once you peel and devein the prawns, you can halve them lengthwise for a lighter presentation.

BEFORE COOKING:

In a large pot, bring to a rolling boil:

4-4.5 litres (6½ -7 pints) water

Add:

500g (1lb) fresh Chinese egg noodles

Cook until softened. Drain. Stir together well in a medium bowl:

1 tsp light or dark soy sauce

1 tsp cornflour

Stir in:

1 tsp toasted sesame oil

Cut across the grain to make very thin 5 x 2.5cm (2 x 1in) slices (easier with partially frozen meat):

250g (8oz) rump steak

Toss in the soy mixture and let marinate for 20 to 30 minutes. Stir together well in another medium bowl:

1 tsp cornflour

1 tsp toasted sesame oil

Peel and devein, 111:

250g (8oz) jumbo prawns

Toss in the cornflour mixture and let marinate for 15 to 20 minutes. Place on a large plate:

30g (1oz) sliced mushrooms

90g (3oz) small bok choy leaves

30g (1oz) sliced bamboo shoots

Stir together well in a small bowl:

250ml (8floz) Chicken Stock, 17

2 tsp light or dark soy sauce

1 tsp salt

1 tsp sugar

Stir together well in a cup, leaving the mixing spoon in for later:

2 tsp cornflour

2 tbsp cool water

Have ready:

½ tsp toasted sesame oil

TO COOK:

Heat a wok or a round-bottomed pan over high heat. When hot, pour in:

125ml (4floz) peanut oil

Swirl around the wok until hot. Add the noodles, heaping them together loosely in a flat mound in the round bottom of the wok. Cook without disturbing until the bottom turns golden brown and the "cake" has become firm. With a slotted spoon or spatula, gently lift the noodle cake out. Invert it onto a serving platter. Keep warm in a very low oven. Heat a clean wok or large frying pan over high heat. When hot, pour in:

3 tbsp peanut oil

Swirl around the wok until very hot but not smoking. Add the beef, quickly stirring and flipping in the oil to separate the slices, and cook lightly. Drain in a sieve or colander. Reheat the wok over high heat. When hot, pour in:

3 tbsp peanut oil

Swirl until very hot but not smoking. Add the prawns and cook, stirring vigorously, until translucent, 30 to 45 seconds. Drain in a sieve or colander. Reheat the wok over high heat. When hot, pour in:

60ml (2floz) peanut oil

Swirl until very hot but not smoking. Add the mushrooms, bok choy and bamboo shoots. Stir and toss vigorously until the vegetables are well coated with oil, about 45 seconds.

Add the chicken stock mixture. Stir occasionally until the mixture boils gently.

Add the beef and prawns. Stir well. Stir the cornflour mixture. Pour slowly into the sauce while stirring. Stir until the mixture is thickened and the contents are glazed and shiny.

Stir in the reserved sesame oil. Pour on top of the noodle "cake". Sprinkle with:

½ tsp cracked black peppercorns

Serve immediately.

Japanese Noodles in Broth

4 to 6 servings

Simplicity itself – freshly cooked noodles in a flavourful broth garnished with spring onions and spices. Cooking the noodles first and then reheating them in boiling water guarantees that they will not get soft sitting in the broth.

BEFORE COOKING:

Have ready:

250g (8oz) 5cm (2in) pieces spring onion

Japanese seven-spice mix (shichimi), available in small shakers in Japanese shops, or Chinese five-spice mix (optional)

TO COOK:

Bring to a rolling boil in a large pot:

3.5-4 litres (6-6½ pints) water

Add and cook until softened:

500g (1lb) dried udon noodles

Drain and rinse under cold water until cool.

Bring to a boil in a large pot over high heat:

2 litres (3¼ pints) Chicken Stock, 17

60ml (2floz) Japanese soy sauce

2 tbsp sugar

1 tbsp salt

The broth can be prepared in advance and refrigerated but must be served boiling hot.

TO SERVE:

Boil a generous amount of water in a large pot. Place the noodles in a sieve and dip them into the boiling water to reheat. Divide the noodles among soup bowls. Sprinkle with the spring onions. Ladle 375-500ml (12-16floz) seasoned broth into each bowl. Sprinkle on the spice mix, if using, to taste.

JAPANESE NOODLES IN DASHI

4 to 6 servings

Prepare *Japanese Noodles in Broth, left,* substituting *Dashi, opposite,* for the stock, seasoned with 5 tbsp Japanese soy sauce, 2 tbsp sugar and 2 tbsp mirin.

MOON-VIEWING NOODLES

4 to 6 servings

Traditionally eaten to celebrate the first full moon in September with the yolk of a poached egg representing the celestial body. Prepare *Japanese Noodles in Broth, left.* Top each bowl with a carefully poached egg.

Dashi

About 1 litre (1½ pints)

One of the bases of traditional Japanese cuisine, this stock is made quickly from just two ingredients – kombu, or kelp, and katsuobushi, or dried bonito flakes (above), also referred to as smoky fish flakes – both of which can be found in Oriental markets or health food shops. Dashi should be used within 4 to 5 days of preparation. It should not be boiled or cooked for too long, and it does not freeze well.

Combine in a stockpot over high heat:

One 12.5 x 10cm (5 x 4in) piece kombu (kelp)

1.1 litres (1¾ pint) cold water

Bring almost to a boil. Immediately remove from the heat and stir in:

5 tbsp loosely packed *katsuobushi* (dried bonito flakes)

Let stand until the flakes begin to sink, 2 to 3 minutes. Remove the kombu with tongs. Strain the stock at once into a clean pot or heatproof plastic container. Let cool, uncovered, then refrigerate until ready to use.

Chicken-Enriched Dashi (Tori-Gara Dashi)

About 1 litre (1½ pints)

Cover with cold water in a stockpot over high heat:

500g (1lb) chicken parts (back, neck, wing, leg, or thigh), well rinsed

Bring to a boil. Immediately drain and rinse the chicken parts and the pot. Return the chicken to the pot with:

One 12.5 x 10cm (5 x 4in) piece kombu (kelp)

1.5 litres (2½ pints) cold water

Bring to a boil, reduce the heat, and simmer gently. Cook, uncovered, skimming often, for 20 to 25 minutes. Season with:

1 tbsp Japanese soy sauce

Remove from the heat and stir in:

5 tbsp *katsuobushi* (dried bonito flakes)

Let stand until the flakes begin to sink, 2 to 3 minutes. Remove the kombu with tongs. Strain the stock into a clean pot or heatproof plastic container. Let cool, uncovered, then refrigerate until ready to use.

KELP, BONITO FLAKES AND JAPANESE SOY SAUCE

Sold as *dashi kombu*, a 185g (6oz) packet of kelp (above) will be enough to make six batches of broth for 4 to 6 people. The whitish coating on kelp is okay. Kelp should never be washed, or it will lose flavour. Kelp keeps indefinitely in a tightly sealed container.

Bonito flakes are dried, salted, fermented fish flakes. They keep indefinitely on a cool, dark shelf.

Japanese soy sauce (*shoyu*) is standard to Japanese cooking and is what they call dark soy sauce, which is labelled *soy sauce, shoyu,* or *koi-kuchi shoyu.* This sauce, on a Chinese scale of dark to light, would fall on the light end, and at a pinch could be substituted for light soy. The Japanese also market low-sodium soy sauces. Like salt, however, it is better to cut back on the amount of this most fundamental seasoning than to use an altered version of it. For more information, please see *Soy Sauce, 95.*

Cold Soba Noodles in a Basket

4 servings

Enjoyed in northern Japan, these thin brownish noodles are made from wheat flour and buckwheat, a hardy plant that grows well in harsh climates. The dried noodles are expensive, but there is no real substitute for their slightly nutty, appealing taste. This is the classic way the Japanese eat their buckwheat noodles – chilled and with spicy condiments, including wasabi, the green horseradish paste familiar to sushi eaters. The noodles are usually served in a small, flat noodle basket or slotted box, but an attractive salad plate works just as well.

BEFORE COOKING:

Combine in a medium saucepan over medium heat:

625ml (1 pint) *Dashi,* **115**

125ml (4floz) plus 2 tbsp Japanese soy sauce

60ml (2floz) mirin

1 tsp sugar

Bring to a gentle boil. Stir in:

185g (6oz) dried bonito flakes (available in Japanese shops)

Remove from the heat. After the flakes are wet, about 15 seconds, strain the liquid and let cool to room temperature. This will keep, covered and refrigerated, for up to 24 hours.

Using scissors, cut into fine shreds and place on a saucer or small plate:

1 sheet nori (a dark, thin sheet of seaweed, available in Japanese shops)

Arrange on a plate:

2 tbsp wasabi paste

60g (2oz) 5cm (2in) pieces spring onion

5 tbsp grated radishes, preferably mooli

TO COOK:

Bring to a rolling boil in a large pot:

2-3 litres (3¼ -5 pints) water

Add and cook until nearly tender:

250g (8oz) dried soba noodles

Drain and rinse under cold water until cool, swishing the noodles with your hand to rinse well.

TO SERVE:

Divide the noodles among 4 baskets, bowls or salad plates. Sprinkle each serving with the nori shreds. Divide the dipping sauce among 4 small bowls and place beside each serving. Place the plate with the wasabi on it within easy reach.

MOOLI

Autumn brings enormous (30cm/12in long) pure white, carrot-shaped, juicy radishes known as *daikon* (above) in Japan, *lo baak* in China and *mooli* in India. Unlike our spring and summer radishes, these white radishes are mild in flavour and a valued part of the daily diet – often pickled, added to soup or grated and cooked with other vegetables and spices.

MIRIN

Sometimes called "sweet sake", mirin is rice wine with an 8 percent alcohol content and loads of sugar. Buy *hon-mirin*, which is naturally brewed and contains natural sugars, if you can find it. *Aji-mirin* is sweetened with corn syrup and may contain other additives. Mirin can be stored indefinitely on a cool, dark shelf.

NORI

Nori are the paper-thin sheets of seaweed used to wrap sushi rolls. Keep nori in the freezer – the sheets thaw almost instantaneously and can be refrozen.

WASABI

Fresh wasabi, a 10-13cm (4-5in) root indigenous to swampy earth next to cold mountain streams in Japan, is rarely available. Powdered wasabi should be mixed, half and half, with tepid water and then allowed to sit for 15 minutes to develop its flavour. Mix a small lump of this pungent green paste with a little soy sauce to make a dip for sushi. Keep in mind that once the packet of wasabi has been opened, it deteriorates quickly. Alternatively, buy in paste form in a tube.

Spicy Pepper Pesto Soba

4 to 6 servings

Soba is a captivating noodle. Widely available today, it cooks in just a few minutes. And once it is cooked, you can toss the noodles with all different types of fresh herb pastes or dressings.

BEFORE COOKING:

Bring to a boil in a medium pot:

2 litres (3¼ pints) water

Add:

2 boneless, skinless chicken breasts

Poach for 5 to 7 minutes. Drain. Let cool, shred and reserve on a saucer or small plate.

Bring to a boil in a medium saucepan:

2 litres (3¼ pints) water

Add and quickly remove 10 to 15 seconds later:

185g (6oz) mange tout, ends trimmed

Rinse immediately under cold water until cool. Place on a plate. Place on the same plate:

1 red pepper, cut into 5cm (2in) thin strips

1 yellow pepper, cut into 5cm (2in) thin strips

Stir together well in a large bowl:

125ml (4floz) Japanese soy sauce

3½ tbsp mirin or sake

3 tbsp Chinese black vinegar or Worcestershire sauce

2½ tbsp sugar

1 tbsp safflower or corn oil

Add the chicken, mange tout and red and yellow pepper strips. Toss to coat thoroughly.

Finely chop in a food processor or blender:

6 cloves garlic, peeled

2 fresh jalapeño chillies, seeded

30g (1oz) fresh coriander leaves

15g (½ oz) fresh parsley leaves

1 tbsp toasted sesame oil

TO COOK:

Bring to a rolling boil in a large pot:

4-4.5 litres (6½ -7 pints) water

Add and cook until nearly tender, 3 to 4 minutes:

375g (12oz) dried soba noodles

Drain and rinse under cold water until cool. Drain. Pour into a large bowl.

Add the garlic mixture to the noodles and toss to coat thoroughly. Stir the chicken and vegetable mixture and arrange attractively on top of the noodles. Serve immediately.

JALAPEÑO CHILLIES

These stubby green to red chillies are widely available and can vary considerably in their heat from totally mild (a new heatless jalapeño is now being grown for use in commercial salsa) to quite hot varieties found in specialist markets and their homeland of Veracruz, Mexico. This chilli's bright green, juicy, grassy taste works well in many dishes, from raw salsas to soups and stews, and even stuffed and fried. When mature jalapeños are smoked and dried, they are known as chipotles. Fresh jalapeños measure about 6cm (2½ in) in length and are 2cm (¾ in) wide at the stem end and taper a little before coming to a rather blunt tip.

ABOUT
DUMPLINGS

*S*imple, satisfying, and a particular treat in cold-weather months, *dumplings take many forms. The word* dumpling *originally meant something that was hollow. This idea of the dumpling still survives today. Modern savoury dumplings, however, are solid, made with a base of flour or cooked potatoes. There are two principal types. European dumplings such as* Nockerln, 122, *and* Spätzle, 123, *as well as the Italian variety known as* Potato Gnocchi, 124, *are similar to fresh pasta in taste and texture. Although these dumplings are sometimes cooked in a soup or stew, they are more commonly simmered in water and then added to a dish or combined with butter or a sauce after they have been fully cooked. American dumplings, by contrast, are light, fluffy and dry, akin to cake. They are cooked on top of a stew, pie or casserole and served directly out of the dish.*

Cornmeal Dumplings, 122

Cooking Dumplings

When cooking dumplings, start with plenty of liquid, as dumplings absorb a lot. The liquid should be simmering when the dumplings are dropped in, and kept at a simmer throughout cooking. Otherwise, the dumplings may become soggy or even disintegrate. You can usually cook European-style dumplings in advance and then add them to a hot stew just before serving. To prevent the dumplings from turning soft and sticky, drain them well, lightly coat them with oil or melted butter and store them in a single layer, covered, in the refrigerator for up to 2 days. American-style dumplings must be served as soon as they are done, or they will become heavy.

Dumplings

6 to 8 servings

These easy-to-make dumplings are the richest and fluffiest we know. They are perfect cooked on top of fricassées and stews.

Mix together:

315g (10oz) plain flour
1 tbsp baking powder
¾ tsp salt

Bring just to a simmer in a small saucepan:

45g (1½ oz) butter
250ml (8floz) milk

Add to the dry ingredients. Stir with a fork or knead by hand 2 to 3 times until the mixture just comes together. Divide the dough into about 18 puffy dumplings. Roll each piece of dough into a rough ball. Gently lay the formed dumplings on the surface of your stew, cover and simmer for 10 minutes. Serve immediately.

Cornmeal Dumplings

4 to 6 servings

Bring to a simmer:

1.25-1.5 litres (2-2½ pints) Brown Beef Stock, 17, or Chicken Stock, 17

Meanwhile, sift together:

125g (4oz) plain flour
60g (2oz) cornmeal
2 tsp baking powder
½ tsp salt

Cut in with a fork or pastry blender:

15g (½ oz) cold butter

Whisk together:

1 large egg
80ml (3oz) milk

Stir into the dry ingredients just until blended. Gently drop teaspoonfuls of the batter into the simmering stock. Tightly cover the pan. Simmer the dumplings for 20 minutes. Serve hot with the stock.

Nockerln

About 250ml (8floz)

An Austrian dumpling, a bit lighter than Spätzle, opposite.

Beat until creamy:

60g (2oz) unsalted butter, softened
1 large egg

Stir in:

155g (5oz) plain flour
⅛ tsp salt

Gradually stir in until a firm batter is formed:

About 6 tbsp milk

Shape teaspoonfuls of the batter into small balls. Drop them into boiling water or directly into the clear soup in which they will be served. Reduce the heat and simmer, covered, for 10 minutes. For a stew, cook the nockerln in water, drain and drop them into the meat mixture just before serving.

Potato Dumplings (Kartoffelklöse)

6 to 8 servings

These are light and tender, especially good with a roast and gravy. They are traditional with sauerbraten, but you could also treat them like Italian gnocchi.

Cook in a large pot of boiling water until tender:

6 medium baking potatoes, unpeeled

When cool enough to handle, peel and mash the potatoes. Combine with:

2 large eggs
75g (2½ oz) plain flour
1½ tsp salt

Beat the batter with a fork until fluffy. Lightly shape into 2.5cm (1in) balls. Bring to a gentle boil in a large pot:

6 litres (10 pints) water
2 tbsp salt

Drop the balls into the water and cook for 10 minutes. Drain. Stir together:

125g (4oz) butter, melted, or bacon dripping
30g (1oz) dry breadcrumbs

Sprinkle the crumbs over the dumplings and serve.

CHEESE SPÄTZLE

Prepare *Spätzle, above,* drain, and remove to a shallow baking dish. Top with 4 tbsp grated mild cheese. Grill until the cheese is melted, about 1 minute.

Spätzle

4 or 5 servings

Spätzle, spätzen, or, more plainly, German egg dumplings are often served alongside a goulash or stew and are particularly welcome next to roast veal. Substituting milk for the water produces a richer, if slightly denser, dumpling. Spätzle are also delicious when pan-seared in a buttered frying pan until the edges are crisp.

Combine:

235g (7½ oz) plain flour
½ tsp baking powder
¾ tsp salt
Pinch of freshly grated or ground nutmeg

Beat together:

2 large eggs
125ml (4floz) milk or water

Add to the flour mixture. Beat well with a wooden spoon to create a fairly elastic batter. Bring to a simmer in a large saucepan:

1.5 litres (2½ pints) salted water or Chicken Stock, 17

Drop small bits of the batter from a spoon into the bubbling liquid, or force the batter through a spätzle machine or colander to produce strands of dough that will puff into irregular shapes. Spätzle are done when they float to the surface. They should be delicate and light, although slightly chewy. If the first few taste heavy and dense, add a few more drops of milk or water to the batter before continuing. Lift the cooked spätzle from the saucepan with a sieve or slotted spoon. Serve spätzle as a side dish, sprinkled with:

Melted butter

Or melt in a small frying pan over medium heat:

15g (½ oz) butter

Add and cook, stirring, until toasted, 3 to 5 minutes:

30g (1oz) fresh breadcrumbs

Sprinkle over the hot spätzle.

Potato Gnocchi

About 80 pieces; 4 to 6 servings

Gnocchi are a pasta for potato lovers and well worth the time and effort invested in baking the potatoes and making and shaping the dough. Make them ahead for a special occasion and bring them out of the freezer just before the guests arrive. For Italians, these chewy bite-sized dumplings are always served as a pasta, cooked and sauced in the same way and eaten as a first course or as a one-dish meal.
Preheat the oven to 200°C (400°F) Gas 6.
Scrub well:

1kg (2lb) baking potatoes
Prick each potato in a dozen places with a fork. Bake directly on an oven rack until easily pierced with a fork, about 1 hour. While the potatoes are still hot, split them lengthwise and scoop out the pulp. Push it through a potato ricer or force through a sieve with the back of a spoon. Combine the potatoes in a bowl with:

200g (7oz) plain flour

1 tsp salt
¼ tsp freshly grated or ground nutmeg
Stir vigorously, then turn out onto a work surface and knead until smooth and blended. Bring 7.5-10cm (3-4in) well-salted water to a simmer in a large pot. Have ready:

45g (1½ oz) butter, melted, or 3 tbsp olive oil
Roll about 2 tablespoons of the dough into a cylinder 2cm (¾ in) wide. Cut it into pieces 2cm (¾ in) long. Roll each piece against the tines of a fork. Drop the gnocchi into the simmering water and cook until they float, about 2 minutes. They should hold a firm shape and be chewy to the bite. If they turn out slimy and soft, knead into the dough:

3 tbsp plain flour
Then test again. When the dough is right, roll it into 3 or 4 ropes 2cm (¾ in) wide, cut the ropes into 2cm (¾ in) pieces, and form the pieces

as gnocchi. Drop one-third to one-half of the gnocchi into the pot and simmer, uncovered, until they float, then remove with a slotted spoon or skimmer to a wide bowl. Drizzle some of the melted butter over the gnocchi. Toss to coat. Repeat until all the gnocchi are done. Serve at once with:

Additional melted butter and grated Parmesan cheese, a tomato sauce or ragù, or *Pesto Sauce*, 52
To make gnocchi ahead, spread the uncooked gnocchi on a lightly floured baking tray and refrigerate, covered with cling film, for up to 12 hours. To keep them longer, freeze the gnocchi on the baking tray until hard, then remove to a freezer bag or container. Gnocchi will keep frozen for up to 1 month. Cook directly from the freezer, adding about 1 minute to the cooking time.

Index

ACKNOWLEDGEMENTS

Special thanks to my wife and editor in residence, Susan; our indispensable assistant and comrade, Mary Gilbert; and our friends and agents, Gene Winick and Sam Pinkus. Much appreciation also goes to Simon & Schuster, Scribner and Weldon Owen for their devotion to this project. Thank you Carolyn, Susan, Bill, Marah, John, Terry, Roger, Gaye, Val, Norman and all the other capable and talented folks who gave a part of themselves to the Joy of Cooking All About series.

My eternal appreciation goes to the food experts, writers, and editors whose contributions and collaborations are at the heart of Joy – especially Stephen Schmidt. He was to the 1997 edition what Chef Pierre Adrian was to Mom's final editions of Joy. Thank you one and all.

Ethan Becker

FOOD EXPERTS, WRITERS, AND EDITORS
Selma Abrams, Jody Adams, Samia Ahad, Bruce Aidells, Katherine Alford, Deirdre Allen, Pam Anderson, Elizabeth Andoh, Phillip Andres, Alice Arndt, John Ash, Nancy Baggett, Rick and Deann Bayless, Lee E. Benning, Rose Levy Beranbaum, Brigit Legere Binns, Jack Bishop, Carole Bloom, Arthur Boehm, Ed Brown, JeanMarie Brownson, Larry Catanzaro, Val Cipollone, Polly Clingerman, Elaine Corn, Bruce Cost, Amy Cotler, Brian Crawley, Gail Damerow, Linda Dann, Deirdre Davis, Jane Spencer Davis, Erica De Mane, Susan Derecskey, Abigail Johnson Dodge, Jim Dodge, Aurora Esther, Michele Fagerroos, Eva Forson, Margaret Fox, Betty Fussell, Mary Gilbert, Darra Goldstein, Elaine Gonzalez, Dorie Greenspan, Maria Guarnaschelli, Helen Gustafson, Pat Haley, Gordon Hamersley, Melissa Hamilton, Jessica Harris, Hallie Harron, Nao Hauser, William Hay, Larry Hayden, Kate Hays, Marcella Hazan, Tim Healea, Janie Hibler, Lee Hofstetter, Paula Hogan, Rosemary Howe, Mike Hughes, Jennifer Humphries, Dana Jacobi, Stephen Johnson, Lynne Rossetto Kasper, Denis Kelly, Fran Kennedy, Johanne Killeen and George Germon, Shirley King, Maya Klein, Diane M. Kochilas, Phyllis Kohn, Aglaia Kremezi, Mildred Kroll, Loni Kuhn, Corby Kummer, Virginia Lawrence, Jill Leigh, Karen Levin, Lori Longbotham, Susan Hermann Loomis, Emily Luchetti, Stephanie Lyness, Karen MacNeil, Deborah Madison, Linda Marino, Kathleen McAndrews, Alice Medrich, Anne Mendelson, Lisa Montenegro, Cindy Mushet, Marion Nestle, Toby Oksman, Joyce O'Neill, Suzen O'Rourke, Russ Parsons, Holly Pearson, James Peterson, Marina Petrakos, Mary Placek, Maricel Presilla, Marion K. Pruitt, Adam Rapoport, Mardee Haidin Regan, Peter Reinhart, Sarah Anne Reynolds, Madge Rosenberg, Nicole Routhier, Jon Rowley, Nancy Ross Ryan, Chris Schlesinger, Stephen Schmidt, Lisa Schumacher, Marie Simmons, Nina Simonds, A. Cort Sinnes, Sue Spitler, Marah Stets, Molly Stevens, Christopher Stoye, Susan Stuck, Sylvia Thompson, Jean and Pierre Troisgros, Jill Van Cleave, Patricia Wells, Laurie Wenk, Caroline Wheaton, Jasper White, Jonathan White, Marilyn Wilkenson, Carla Williams, Virginia Willis, John Willoughby, Deborah Winson, Lisa Yockelson.

Weldon Owen wishes to thank the following people and organizations for their generous assistance and support in producing this book: Desne Border, Ken DellaPenta, Sharilyn Hovind, Lucca Ravioli Company and Joan Olson.